★★★★★★★★★★★★★★★★★★★★★★★★

10

Steps to Repair American Democracy

★★★★★★★★★★★★★★★★★★★★★★★★

Also by Steven Hill

Fixing Elections: The Failure of America's Winner Take All Politics
(www.FixingElections.com)

Whose Vote Counts?
(with Robert Richie)

★★★★★★★★★★★★★★★★★★★★★★★★★★★★★★★★★★★★★★★

10
Steps to Repair
American
Democracy

★★★★★★★★★★★★★★★★★★★★★★★★★★★★★★★★★★★★★★★

Steven Hill

★★★★★★★★★★★★★★★★★★★★★★★★★★★★★★★★★★★★★★★

Foreword by Hendrik Hertzberg

PoliPointPress

10 Steps to Repair American Democracy
by Steven Hill

This edition published in 2006 in the United States of America by
PoliPointPress, P.O. Box 3008, Sausalito, CA 94966
www.PoliPointPress.org

Production management: Michael Bass Associates
Book design: Linda M. Robertson, LMR Designs
Cover design: Greg Flejtuch

Library of Congress Cataloging-In-Publication Data

Hill, Steven
10 Steps to Repair American Democracy / Steven Hill; foreword by
Hendrik Hertzberg.

ISBN: 0-9760621-5-1

Library of Congress Control Number: 2005910607

Printed in the United States of America
February 2006

Published by:
PoliPointPress, LLC
P.O. Box 3008
Sausalito, CA 94966-3008
(415) 339-4100
www.PoliPointPress.org

Distributed by Publishers Group West

For my parents,
Pat and Jack Hill

Contents

Foreword

by Hendrik Hertzberg

Americans and politics: It's the ultimate love-hate relationship.

On one side, our sentiments about our political arrangements—that is, about our Constitution, not only the written
document but also the institutions and customs and practices en-
crusted around it—go beyond love to outright worship. Ancestor
worship, even. We consult the Constitution of the United States
and the Federalist Papers—the Pentateuch and Talmud of our
civic religion—as the ultimate repositories of political revelation,
eternally valid for every age and circumstance and incapable of
improvement. Our founders—excuse me, Founders—were all-
seeing, all-knowing, godlike. What other nation has a capital city
named for one long-ago politician and dominated by temples
dedicated to the quasi-deification of others? We are, our leaders
endlessly assure us, the greatest nation on Earth. Therefore, our
institutions and practices, which make us what we are, must be the
greatest institutions and practices on Earth. End of discussion.

Lucky us! Except that we do nothing but complain, and our
complaints, oddly, all seem to have to do with our institutions
and practices. We hate politics. Politics is crooked; it's fixed; it's
dominated by money; it's manipulated by special interests; it's
shot through with dishonesty and pandering and betrayal and ir-
responsibility. And we don't like politicians much, either—living
ones, anyway. (The dead ones, after a suitable interval, become
demigods.) We revere our institutions, but we scorn the people who
comprise them. We scorn them because they're out of touch.
Why don't they give us what we want? We scorn them because all
they think about is getting reelected. Why don't they have the
courage to defy the opinion polls? They must be especially wicked

to have screwed things up so badly, because, after all, they start out with the advantage of being embedded in the greatest institutions on Earth. They're hopeless. It's hopeless. So we're hopeless.

Americans are right to revere the Founding Fathers. The machine they put together in Philadelphia in 1789 was a small miracle, maybe even a large one. At the time, it was the most advanced, most cutting-edge, and probably the most "democratic"—even if the Constitution's authors didn't use or even much like the word—system of government on Earth. But, by the same token, the stagecoach was the most advanced form of land transportation on Earth. Free government, even more than efficient transportation, remains a crucial goal. But shouldn't technological advances be taken advantage of?

After the 2000 election, when, for the first time in the modern democratic era, the United States ended up with a president who had received fewer votes than his principal opponent, it dawned on many Americans that our political technology was so outdated that it had begun to undermine our political ideals. There was widespread indignation about chaos and disfranchisement, accidental and purposeful, in Florida. Commissions issued reports calling for various modest reforms. But the problems go deeper than hanging chads and sloppy voter rolls, and a growing minority of Americans has begun to realize it.

Around the world, democracy has never been more popular or prevalent than it is today. But when new democracies emerge, as they did in the 1990s from Prague to Pretoria, the American model, apart from the Bill of Rights, is almost universally rejected. The international trend is decisively away from American-style winner-take-all elections. No one has adopted our Electoral College method of executive selection. No new democracy has invested its upper chamber with the degree of power we bestow on our grossly unrepresentative Senate. We find ourselves in the middle of an embarrassing paradox: As the U.S. government strives to spread democracy to places like the Middle East, fewer and fewer favor our institutions and practices.

Our geographically based, plurality winner-take-all method of representation serves us especially poorly. It's why control of the House and the Senate is decided in a dozen districts and a half-dozen states; and in those districts and states, the issues don't necessarily cut the way they do in the country at large. If a position that might win millions of extra votes in New York and California—strong gun control, say, or tougher environmental protection—will cost your party a few thousand votes in West Virginia, it isn't worth it. So Democrats stick to Social Security and Medicare, Republicans stick to terrorism and tax cuts, both sides stick to negative attacks, and the general public wonders why "real issues" aren't being "addressed."

The presidential election works much the same way—badly. Political insiders knew months before the 2004 election that the winner would be decided in two states, Ohio and Florida—just as it was in 2000, and just as it will be in 2008. It is only a slight exaggeration to say that in the other 48 states, presidential politics above the primary level is moribund. Our method for electing a president ensures that Republican and Democratic voters in only about a dozen states have any chance of playing a direct role in the selection of their respective parties' candidates for national office. As for general elections, most states are locked up for one side or the other as far into the future as the eye can see. Most voters treat the presidential election as if it were a soap opera or sporting event on TV—and, for them, that's all it can be. Turnout is abysmal, but the wonder isn't that it's so low. It's that it's so high. In most places, voting simply isn't a meaningful political act.

To ponder the shortcomings of our political system is to court despondency. But acknowledging the underlying dysfunctionality of our political institutions and practices has powerful therapeutic value. If we kept in mind the ways in which our political institutions distort our democracy and hobble our politics, we might gain a deeper, more useful understanding of the sources of our various national discontents. If we didn't assume that our political system was perfect, we wouldn't assume that everything we don't like is the fault of bad people. We'd judge our politicians more shrewdly—and more charitably—if we reminded ourselves regularly of the perverse incentives that our antiquated system imposes on them. We'd be less tempted by lazy moralism and more interested in sensible reform.

So we are fortunate to have Steven Hill's latest book, *10 Steps to Repair American Democracy*, to help us find our political compass. He identifies 10 critical problems with our democracy and offers concrete solutions to each one. He outlines ways to allow more people to vote and to make sure voting equipment counts our ballots properly. He proposes that we replace winner-take-all elections with alternative methods that give better representation and encourage constructive debate and coalition building rather than scorched-earth tactics. He recommends that presidents be elected by, of all things, the democratic vote of the people. He proposes reforms for the Senate, which increasingly exaggerates the power of sparsely populated conservative "red" states, and for the Supreme Court, which now resembles an unelected legislature where, as he writes, "five votes beats a reason any day." And he promotes the advantages of publicly financed elections, free media time for candidates, and media reforms that will produce a more balanced approach to the media's public interest responsibilities. By identifying urgent problems and proposing specific solutions, Hill provides the busy, concerned citizen not only with a concise, comprehensive overview but also with a sense of how to parse the big picture into smaller bite-sizes suitable for activism. *10 Steps* is a blueprint for a reinvigoration of our republic.

Hill shows that there actually is a way we can keep faith with our Founding Fathers. And it's not to pretend that the particular political improvisations and compromises they came up with more than two centuries ago—brilliant and clever though they were in the context of their times—provide the answer to every question. No, the way to honor the Founders is not to worship them. It's to imitate them. It's to do what they did: Diagnose what's wrong; be fearless about innovation; learn from experience; design political mechanisms with a view to taking account of human imperfection and marshaling the self-interest of politicians for the common good. The question isn't, What, way back when, did Jefferson (and Madison and Hamilton) do? The question is, What would they do now? The answers begin here.

Introduction:
America's Faltering Republic[1]

Only a crisis—actual or perceived—produces real change.
When that crisis occurs, the actions that are taken depend on
the ideas that are lying around. That, I believe, is our basic function:
to develop alternatives to existing policies, to keep them alive and available
until the politically impossible becomes politically inevitable.

—MILTON FRIEDMAN[2]

Despite their impassioned efforts over the past decade, both the Republican and Democratic parties have failed to galvanize the American citizenry around a vision or program capable of uniting the nation. Instead, the two major parties have emerged as a kind of twin-headed monster, with much of what passes for politics having degenerated into a partisan brew of spin, scandal, name-calling, money chasing, and pandering. Rather than expanding their voter bases, the two parties are shedding supporters as more Americans than ever become hostile to them. That's because both parties have allowed themselves to be taken hostage by their own narrow pressure groups and special interests, including religious fundamentalists, America First unilateralists, corporate lobbyists, and free market ideologues in the case of the Republican Party; and an octopus of single-issue groups, poll-obsessed

1

strategists, and Hollywood and limousine liberals in the case of the Democratic Party.

The influence of the extremes has alienated growing numbers of Americans from both parties. For while the right wing of the Republican Party and the liberal wing of the Democratic Party have become more dominant within their parties, the American people themselves have remained moderate in their views.[3] A national poll during the 2000 election revealed that 50 percent of Americans view themselves as moderate, substantially more than the number who describe themselves as either conservative (29 percent) or liberal (20 percent).[4] In the states that register voters by party, the number of independent voters has increased 300 percent over the last decade, and a Gallup poll found 37 percent of respondents self-identified as independent, more than either party.[5] Among younger Americans, 18 to 29 years old, 44 percent are independents compared to only 29 percent Democrats and 26 percent Republicans.[6] A 2005 Zogby poll found that 70 percent of Americans believe both the Democrat and Republican parties should be broad based and pursue compromise yet are too focused on their respective base voters, making compromise impossible.[7] Most Americans today, when they bother to vote at all, vote *against* one side or the other rather than *for* a candidate or a political party they believe in. Increasingly, the American mainstream is reacting with alienation and even disgust toward their political leadership.

Despite many Americans' political freelancing and apparent moderation, recent electoral maps suggest that the United States is torn into a disunited hodgepodge of red and blue political fiefdoms. These maps also indicate a striking regional component to our disunity: The Democrats dominate the cities, the coasts, and most parts of the Midwest and New England; the Republicans dominate the rural regions and the vast flyover zones of the South and the West (except the West Coast). Liberals and conservatives are clustering in their own partisan residential enclaves, which, as we shall see, has enormous ramifications for our politics. Moreover, demographic studies reveal stark racial and cultural dimensions to this regional partisan geography: whites and religious conservatives vote mostly for Republicans (or against Democrats, as the case may be); racial minorities and secular voters vote for Democrats (or against Republicans).

How can we account for this seeming contradiction between a preponderance of moderate and independent voters, on the one hand, and deep partisan divisions, on the other? It's simple: Our antiquated political system forces us into these two hostile factions. Because we elect one district representative at a time in "winner-take-all" contests, only one side wins each individual contest, and all other sides lose. Each district is crowned either red or blue, even though many liberals live in those red districts and many conservatives in the blue districts. Also, there are many moderates, independents, and third party supporters living in all these districts, but they are geographic minorities who rarely win representation in a winner-take-all system. Consequently, moderate and independent representatives, who traditionally have acted as the bridge builders in legislatures between the political extremes, are going the way of the dodo bird. "Purple America"—neither red nor blue, but a mixture of both— faces an increasingly barren choice.

Sometime in the mid-1990s, we became a "49–49 nation"— roughly the percentage of the vote each major party wins in high-profile elections. Yet this near parity has not led to compromise and cooperation but to rancor and division. With the two sides so closely matched, the ante has been raised, and the tactics have been intensified. Both sides are looking for any advantage in the bruising, partisan combat—even if it imperils our republic. But increasingly this is a no-win proposition. As one recalls the many bare-knuckle battles of the past decade—the Iraq war, *Bush v. Gore*, impeachment, Supreme Court nominations, Terry Schiavo, the Cuban boy Elian Gonzalez, resignation of two House Speakers, and more—one can't help but wonder about the future of our nation. But there is hope. As this book will show, such polarization

3

and political dysfunction are grotesquely exaggerated by the continued use of our once-revolutionary but now-antiquated political institutions. The methods we use to elect the Congress and the president are at the root of what ails our politics. And we don't have to put up with these outdated methods any longer.

"IT'S NOT WHO VOTES THAT COUNTS, BUT WHO COUNTS THE VOTES"

But more than our 18th-century political institutions are failing us. Even the nuts and bolts of election administration are breaking down. With the two sides essentially tied and major elections breathtakingly close, election mechanics have become front-page news. Now, when election administration messes up or faulty equipment breaks down, we notice it. The partisanship of election officials and the companies selling voting equipment suddenly matter. Likewise, the design of a ballot, such as the notorious butterfly ballot that misled thousands of voters in Palm Beach County to vote for Pat Buchanan instead of Al Gore, is no longer negligible.[8]

Respected computer experts have warned that computerized voting is subject to all-too-familiar malfunctions and viruses— not to mention tampering and fraud. It turns out there is more security, oversight, and testing of slot machines and the gaming industry than of the nation's voting equipment or election administration. Numerous irregularities in both the 2004 and 2000 presidential elections have raised more questions than answers. True, the National Research Commission on Elections and Voting, a panel composed of top elections scholars, found no conclusive proof of a stolen election in the 2004 presidential vote. But the commission found "pervasive breakdowns in election administration and oversight" that threaten the credibility of America's electoral process and "make it impossible to definitively put theories and accusations of fraud to rest."[9] In other words, for the second presidential election in a row we could not guarantee the correct candidate had won. Former president Jimmy Carter, who helps monitor elections around the world, refused to monitor the 2004 presidential election in Florida because he said "some basic international requirements for a fair election are missing," namely nonpartisan election officials and uniformity in voting procedures.[10] And that's disturbing.

Like Florida's hanging chads in 2000, the 2004 election became another national Rorschach test that allowed partisans to see whatever they wanted to see, further damaging our ability to achieve national consensus and to serve as an international example of free and fair elections.

THE WEAKENING PULSE OF DEMOCRACY

Other aspects of the American republic also are displaying signs of fatigue. While voter turnout increased in the 2004 presidential election, turnout continues to drop for most other races. On that measure, we are currently ranked 138th in the world—sandwiched between Armenia and Nigeria.[11] Turnout at the local level, and even at state and federal levels, sometimes has fallen to *single digits*.[12] Over 50 million eligible voters—nearly a third of the electorate—are unregistered, a lower percentage than Iraqi voters.[13]

But why should we expect anything different when there is so little electoral competition? In the 2004 elections a mere 6 percent of U.S. House seats were considered up for grabs, and more than 82 percent were won by huge landslide margins. Only five challengers defeated incumbents (in the 2002 House elections only four incumbents lost, the fewest in history). In the presidential election, only 12 states were considered competitive. Many pundits, myself included, predicted six months in advance that George W. Bush's reelection would be decided in Ohio or Florida, an effective battleground of two states. In recent years, 40 percent of over 7,000 state legislative races have had no candidate from one of the two major parties, nearly 3,000 races lacking even nominal campaigning or political debate. Unsurprisingly, various studies have shown that as the level of competition decreases, so does voter turnout, often by dramatic amounts.[14]

The typical explanations for the lack of competition are the need for campaign finance reform and redistricting abuses (e.g., incumbents drawing their own legislative district lines). Both are real problems, but not the core problem. Certainly there are some states where partisan line drawing has unfairly tilted the playing field, such as the GOP gerrymanders in states such as Texas, Florida, Ohio, Pennsylvania, and Michigan.[15] But the main problem is even more basic—it's where people live. New research shows that in most states the previously mentioned partisan residential patterns are even more influential in deciding election outcomes than partisan gerrymanders or campaign spending inequities. Liberals and conservatives are living in their own demographic clusters, and as a result entire regions and states have become one-party fiefdoms. Most districts are branded either Republican red or Democratic blue before the partisan line drawers sit down at their computers and begin drawing their squiggly lines. Partisan residential patterns are outstripping the ability of the line drawers or campaign finance reformers to affect the outcome of most elections.

These partisan residential patterns are exaggerated by the winner-take-all electoral method we use, which elects one representative at a time. On the other's turf, it is impossible for the geographic minority—even when one of the major parties—to win any elections, leading not only to a loss of political competition but also to a loss of debate, a loss of choice for voters, and a drop-off in voter turnout. We think of ours as a two-party system, but increasingly most voters live in a one-party district or state, where their only political choice is to ratify the sole candidate of the party that dominates their region. That's a level of "choice" we expected in the old Soviet Union. Yet it is resulting primarily from partisan residential patterns—where people live—and not from redistricting abuses or campaign finance inequities, as many political analysts have assumed.

This state of affairs points to a jarring contradiction: As the battle between the two major political parties intensifies, the competition in thousands of individual races across the national landscape has become negligible. That's because we don't even have a two-party system anymore in most regions of the country. Like other large winner-take-all democracies such as India and Canada, a most uncivil sectionalism is now a permanent feature of the American political landscape. And that factor does not augur well for our national future.

We must face another fact: Our "representative" government remains stubbornly unrepresentative. John Adams, Founding Father and second president of the United States, once wrote about the U.S. House of Representatives, "This representative assembly . . . should be in miniature an exact portrait of the people at large."[16] Yet today, leaning over the balcony overlooking the chamber of the House of Representatives, a spectator can see that this "People's House" doesn't look very much like "the people." There are a lot of guys down there (about 85 percent) and a lot of white faces (about 84 percent), even though the American population is over 50 percent female and 29 percent minority.[17] There are also a lot of gray hairs and shiny pink pates down there—nobody that looks like, say, an LA hip-hop artist, or a regular at a local Midwest diner, or the waitress who serves her or him, or a Bronx bus-riding commuter. Also, we know there are a lot of lawyers down there, and a lot of businessmen—taken together, perhaps 60 percent of the House membership—and plenty of millionaires.[18]

No, the People's House still doesn't look like the people, hardly at all, and the Senate is even worse in that regard. Out of 100 senators, there are only 14 women and five minorities. Income disparities between most senators and their voters are huge. A 19th-century aphorism said, "It is harder for a poor man to enter the United States Senate than for a rich man to enter

Heaven," and things hardly seem different today despite over 200 years of litigation, activism, protest, sacrifice, blood, lynchings and tears. And of course only white men have been president, and great wealth often has been a prerequisite for that office, too. State legislatures are not much better. No, over 200 years into our history, it is shocking how little the face of the American government has changed. Our representative chambers at federal and state levels are still fairly patrician bodies, more resembling the Roman Senate than a New England town meeting. The unrepresentative reality of our "representative" bodies is an ongoing reminder of how much work still remains.

THE LOSS OF POLITICAL IDEAS:
Media Concentration, Empty Campaigns, and the National Security Media

Besides the ability to hold free and fair elections that produce representative government, a modern democracy requires robust political debate about the pressing issues of our times. Broad public access to the media is the most effective vehicle for encouraging political debate among wide masses of people. Yet American democracy is being threatened by increasing levels of media concentration and ownership by huge, transnational media corporations. By 2000, the U.S. media system was dominated by fewer than 10 giant conglomerates owning a staggering array of media properties, including NBC, CBS, ABC, MTV, Fox News, CNN, Turner Broadcasting, ESPN, America Online, *Time* magazine, and more. In the radio sector, corporate broadcaster Clear Channel has grown from 40 stations to over 1,200 today. Concentration of broadcasters has resulted in canned programming and a loss of local content that have undercut the media's public service mission.

Media concentration has additional negative impacts on our political process. In the absence of either a vigorous public broadcasting sector (such as the British Broadcasting Corporation) or public financing of political campaigns, the corporate media have become gatekeepers of a candidates' viability, especially in high-profile races such as president, governor, or Congress. Successful candidates are vetted by media executives who preselect which candidates may have access to American's TV sets and living rooms. Independent and third party candidates such as Ralph Nader and Pat Buchanan are shut out of presidential debates, as are third party candidates all over the United States, with the exception of a multimillionaire such as Ross Perot. The media gatekeepers also have a veto over which issues will be discussed during the electoral season and the interim periods. Thus, voters are limited to hearing from a narrow range of viewpoints and candidates with either a sizable personal fortune or access to great amounts of wealth. In the 2004 presidential election, candidates John Kerry and George W. Bush both were so independently wealthy that Fox News commentator Bill O'Reilly was prompted to say, "This is a presidential election between two silver spooners."[19]

So, while the United States trumpets the advantages of economic competition and consumer choice, when it comes to our politics, we suffer from an appalling lack of competition and choice. Both presidential campaigns in 2004 were fund-raising vacuum cleaners, setting new spending records of $1.7 billion, nearly twice the amount spent in 2000.[20] Yet Americans hardly were more informed about the full range of issues that confront our nation. For all the billions spent, politicians and their hired-gun campaign consultants used the money to produce McCampaigns of poll-tested blandness and pit bull hack attacks via 30-second ads and sound bites. A few years ago former president Gerald Ford bluntly characterized modern elections in an address to the National Press Club as "candidates without ideas, hiring consultants without convictions, to run campaigns without content."[21] Campaign technologies such as polling and focus groups are central to this race to the bottom, having become the steroids of politics—once one side is using them and gains a competitive edge, the other side doesn't dare not use them.

Since September 11, a new media threat has emerged from what can only be termed the "national security media"—a disturbing overlap between national security interests and compliance of "embedded journalists" who have willingly censored the news. In its most extreme form, journalists Armstrong Williams and Maggie Gallagher (and who knows how many others) were covertly paid to espouse a conservative viewpoint without disclosing the financial arrangements. The U.S. military was caught red-handed, covertly paying Iraqi newspapers to print pro-American propaganda and secretly paying monthly stipends to Iraqi journalists.[22] Less brazen has been the type of "insider" journalism practiced by *New York Times* reporter Judith Miller and the *Washington Post*'s Bob Woodward. Miller in particular misled the country to war by dutifully reporting whatever her anonymous Pentagon and Iraqi exile sources told her about weapons of mass destruction and the like, nearly all of which turned out to be bunk. Her shoddy reporting and that of others eventually prompted the *New York Times* to issue a national apology in May 2004 over its pre–Iraq war coverage.[23]

But the *Times* looked downright unpatriotic compared to the cheerleaders at Fox News. When CNN's top war correspondent, Christiane Amanpour, criticized the press and stated that CNN "was intimidated by the Bush administration and its foot soldiers at Fox News," which cast "a climate of fear and self-censorship," Fox News spokeswoman Irena Briganti responded, as if on cue, "Given the choice, it's better to be viewed as a foot soldier for Bush than a spokeswoman for al Qaeda."[24] The media have so failed in their fulcrum duty of investigating the truth and informing the public that it is difficult for Americans to learn what really is happening in the world or even in the United States without regularly consulting non-American news sources such as the BBC or European newspapers via the World Wide Web.

With the means for political communication in the hands of giant corporations exhibiting a willingness to censor the news for national security purposes, and a lack of a robust public broadcasting sector to take up the slack, and a lack of public financing for candidates, combined with the use of campaign technologies designed to manipulate voters, it should be hardly surprising that the United States is experiencing an astonishing loss of political ideas. Voters are not challenged or stimulated to think deeply about many of the great issues of our times—economic security, health care, our energy future, globalization, global warming, homelessness—because these issues are left mostly on the political sidelines. And the issues like war and terrorism that are discussed are done in such a simplistic sound bite fashion that they contribute little to our understanding of complex matters. Fostering understanding and debate of important issues is simply not the way you win elections today. Likewise, national policy—indeed, our national direction, our national political maturation—has become stunted because it has been deprived of the opportunity to find a consensus via a fully informed debate in the marketplace of ideas.

UNRESPONSIVE GOVERNMENT

You are the Rulers and the Ruled.
—from a ceiling fresco in the Hall of Capitals, U.S. Capitol building

When you step back and look at the big picture, it becomes clear that our rusty old practices and institutions of representative democracy, many dating from the 18th century, are breaking down so often that it nearly defies our ability to catalogue them. Given this breakdown in our basic political institutions, not surprisingly a February 2005 survey revealed how unresponsive and out of tune the American government has become to the priorities of most Americans—even Republicans.

In a poll conducted by the Program on International Policy Attitudes, both Republican and Democratic poll participants said they would take the budget axe to spending on defense and on Iraq and Afghanistan, plowing more funds into education, job training, deficit reduction, homeland security, veterans, the environment, and ways to reduce U.S. reliance on oil. Defense spending would receive the deepest cuts, around $134 billion. Even Republicans opted to cut the defense budget and increase spending for the environment, job training, and the United Nations. Some 63 percent of respondents said they favored rolling back tax cuts for people with incomes in excess of $200,000. The largest reassignment of tax dollars went to social spending, with education increased $26.8 billion and respondents proposing a boost in job training and employment programs by $19 billion (263 percent). Veterans' benefits were raised $12.5 billion, homeland security received an increase of $10.5 billion, and housing was buttressed with a 31 percent increase, or $9.3 billion. The largest percentage increase was for conserving and developing renewable energy—a boost of 1,090 percent, or $24 billion, supported by 70 percent of respondents.

These changes proposed by both Republican and Democratic respondents amounted to a major redirection of the Bush administration's budget. "The American public as a whole takes a fairly coherent position," said survey director Steven Kull. "They favor redirecting a portion of defense spending to deficit reduction and social spending and look for savings by cutting spending on large-scale Cold War style capabilities."[25]

These findings about misplaced priorities are consistent with those of other researchers and studies. The *Financial Times* reported that, according to U.S. Census figures, even as the economy grew in 2004, the real median household income declined by $1,700 compared to 2000, the first time on record that household incomes had failed to increase for five straight years.[26] Lacking sufficient income, more American workers have had to go deeper in debt. Consumer indebtedness has now soared to nearly $11 trillion, and outstanding balances on credit cards have risen to $7,200 per U.S. household, more than double the indebtedness of a decade ago.[27] The number of Americans without health insurance in 2004 climbed for the fourth consecutive year to a record high of 45.8 million people (15.7 percent of the nation), and the poverty rate increased to 37 million (12.7 percent). The *Wall Street Journal* reported that, contrary to widespread belief, researchers have documented that economic mobility in the United States is now less than in "old Europe."[28] That's a very poor showing three years into an economic recovery, where only the top 5 percent have seen their incomes improve. Misplaced priorities and unresponsive government resulting from a poorly functioning democracy are at the root of this inequity.

An American Political Science Association task force examined the causes and consequences of this gap between Americans and their government. In their report, the political scientists wrote that "our government is becoming less democratic, responsive mainly to the privileged, and not a powerful instrument to correct disadvantages or to look out for the majority."[29] The task force expressed deep concern that the voices of the poor, minorities, and average working Americans are getting shut out of politics. This reality was underscored dramatically by the tragic devastation wrought by Hurricane Katrina in New Orleans and along the Gulf Coast, when the whole world viewed on their TV screens the plight of America's urban poor, most of them black, clinging for survival while the better-off and predominantly white people fled to safety. This disaster exposed not only the severe racial and class divisions simmering beneath the surface of most cities, but also the failure of the American system to respond in a way that could help its most vulnerable citizens.

As American government tumbles over the edge, the widespread appreciation for democracy itself is atrophying, like shriveled grapes on a vine. After 30 years of ideological attack by conservatives who have painted government as "the problem" rather than as a vehicle for potential solutions, the public's confidence has waned. Thus, this right-wing ideological attack on government has formed the philosophical underpinnings for an attack on representative democracy itself. For if Americans don't value government, then why should they value democracy, the means and methods used to select our political leaders?

The practice of democracy always has been a contested terrain in the United States, with deep philosophical roots about not only the nature of American democracy but also the role of government. President Richard Nixon crudely expressed one dominant view when, in the privacy of the Oval Office, he sneered, "You got people voting now—blacks, whites, Mexicans and the rest—that shouldn't have anything to say about government; mainly because they don't have the brains to know."[30] A more sophisticated version has appeared more recently, one of its most articulate proponents being Judge Richard Posner, an influential conservative who argues that representative democracy is not about popular empowerment or self-government but largely a matter of elite decision making, with only occasional public ratification necessary.[31]

But this view of elite rule comports closely with that held by many of our political ancestors. The Framers' foresight, which was considerable, nevertheless was the product of an 18th-century understanding about who should vote, how politics should be organized, and how best to hold government accountable. They accepted the odious institution of slavery and the second-class citizenship of women, and they promoted or at least tolerated views of the franchise that are insupportable today. The Framers put a short leash on what they saw as "too much democracy" and burdened us with undemocratic, now-antiquated political institutions such as the U.S. Senate and the Electoral College as a way to contain the popular will. John Jay, Founding Father and first Chief Justice, expressed an all-too-typical attitude when he stated that the upper classes "were the better kind of people, by which I mean the people who are orderly and industrious." His theory of government was simple: "The people who own the country ought to govern it."[32] The consequences of their choices still afflict us today, making it easier for today's gatekeepers, the defenders of elite rule, to maintain a political system that is trickle-down by design.

So while the Bush administration is busy trying to export democracy all over the world, our own republic seems brittle, weary, fragile. For lack of fresh ideas, effective policy informed by spirited debate, competitive elections, a truly representative Congress that is guided by broad-based considerations, and a diverse menu of compelling candidates who can appeal to various constituencies, our political respiration is registering a flat line on the oscilloscope. Most voters have become bystanders in the process, with not only decreasing participation but also declining expectations. And as average Americans come to believe that they don't matter, they become increasingly likely to disengage, leaving the field to the party apparatchiks, operatives, and extremists.

Our nation has reached a critical moment. What is at stake is nothing less than what kind of society we will become—one that works for the broad majority of people? Or one that is captured by a dominant political and economic elite? There's no question that our antiquated political institutions, many of them dating from the 18th century, are not up to the task before us. They must be changed, updated, and, in some cases, ripped out by the roots and replaced.

THE WAY FORWARD

It is time for Americans to take back our representative democracy and government. Two hundred years after our national birth-quake, "government of, by, and for the people" remains an unfulfilled promise. Fortunately, there is another way, a better way, that can lead us toward a brighter national future.

It involves fundamental change to our basic political and media institutions, bringing them into the 21st century instead of leaving them stranded in past centuries. As the U.S. government casts further adrift from the American mainstream, the "politically impossible will become the politically inevitable," to paraphrase economist Milton Friedman. As Friedman wrote, "when that crisis occurs, the actions that are taken depend on the ideas that are lying around." That, I believe, is our task: to develop alternatives to existing democratic practices, to make them available until the politically impossible becomes politically inevitable. That day is looming closer with each passing election.

But what kind of political change will revitalize the United States of America? That is the subject of this book—a blueprint for renewing the American republic. In the following chapters, I will highlight 10 essential steps that can repair and modernize American democracy. I believe these are commonsense changes, most of them already working in other democracies and in some parts of the United States. Some of these reforms will be easier to enact than others; a few of the most important will take more time as they require constitutional amendments. But that should not dissuade us because we have no choice. Without the enactment of these reforms, the great American republic will continue to decline. We have nothing to lose and everything to gain in our patient endeavors.

I'm certain that the Founders and Framers of our nation, being the enlightened rationalists that they were, would have applauded efforts to modernize their political creation and make it into one that lives up to the lofty rhetoric and aspirations of their astonishing age:

> We the People of the United States, in Order to form a more perfect Union, establish Justice, insure domestic Tranquility, provide for the common defence, promote the general Welfare, and secure the Blessings of Liberty to ourselves and our Posterity. . . .

The task before us of remaking American democracy is an epic challenge. The brightness of our national future depends on our success. But Americans have risen to great challenges before, and I believe we will again.

1

Secure the Vote

Election administration is our nation's crazy aunt in the attic. Every few years she pops out and creates a scene, and everyone swears that something must be done. But as soon as Election Day passes, we're happy to ignore her again—until the next time she makes a spectacle of herself.[1]

There has been much discussion since the 2000 election on voting equipment and election administrative practices, but little real action. Like everything else having to do with politics today, this issue has gotten entangled in the partisan war. As a result, what should be a national dialogue about fairness and ensuring every vote is counted is now another shouting match. It has become difficult for the average person to separate fact from fiction, hyperbole and hysteria, from the real causes for alarm.

There's no question that, under a fair, equitable, and democratic system of voting, Al Gore would have been elected president in 2000, and George W. Bush would still be whacking weeds in Crawford, Texas. Butterfly ballots, hanging chads, and the aborted recounts cannot disguise the fact that more people in Florida intended to vote for Gore than Bush, but along the way something happened to their vote. A comprehensive Caltech-MIT study found that ballots from approximately six million voters nationwide—nearly 6 percent of the total—were never counted due to faulty voting machines, poorly designed ballots, polling place failures, long lines, or foul-ups with registration or absentee voting. "This study shows that the voting problem is much worse than we expected," said Caltech president David

Baltimore. "It is remarkable that we in America put up with a system where as many as six out of every hundred voters are unable to get their vote counted. Twenty-first-century technology should be able to do much better than this."[2]

In 2004, we repeated some of the same blunders from 2000. It was as if we hadn't learned a thing. Even though Bush won the national popular vote by some three million ballots, the election was tarnished. In Ohio, the state that decided the election and Bush won by fewer than 120,000 votes, the number of complaints about voting irregularities numbered in the hundreds. Many of those complaints were significant. Approximately 92,000 ballots failed to record a vote for president, even in precincts where voters waited in line for hours to vote—most of them on the same type of discredited punch card systems that malfunctioned in Florida in 2000.[3] Ohio election officials improperly disqualified tens of thousands of the 153,000 provisional ballots cast, especially in places such as Cleveland with high numbers of Democratic voters.[4] In Youngstown, electronic machines transferred an unknown number of votes from Kerry to Bush.[5] In one precinct in Franklin County, Ohio, a computerized voting system recorded 4,258 votes for Bush and 260 votes for Kerry—in a precinct in which only 638 votes were cast (these glitches were corrected).[6] Miami County reported an improbable turnout of 98 percent of registered voters, overwhelmingly strong for Bush.[7]

Most egregiously, voters in many African American precincts waited outside in long lines at polling places for seven, eight, nine hours or more, in nasty weather, due to shortages of voting machines. Old women leaned heavily on walkers, and some people walked out, complaining their bosses would not excuse their lateness. Students at Ohio State University and Kenyon College also waited for nine hours or more in long lines, standing in the rain. Both groups were known to be solid Kerry supporters.[8] But voters in whiter and wealthier precincts, which also had robust voter turnout and favored Bush, oddly had no such shortages of voting machines and could vote in 15 minutes. One study of Franklin County found that wards with the most machines per registered voter showed majorities for Bush, and the wards with the fewest machines delivered large margins for Kerry. In heavily Democratic Columbus alone, bipartisan estimates say that 5,000 to 15,000 frustrated voters turned away without casting ballots.[9]

This kind of discrepancy called to mind Florida in 2000, where precincts in poorer counties—mostly African American—disproportionately were saddled with crummy equipment, resulting in more hanging chads and breakdowns and more of their votes not counting. So was the lack of equipment in Ohio and other discrepancies more evidence of slick skullduggery by Republican operatives to manipulate the vote?

Maybe yes, maybe no. It turns out that all Ohio counties had bipartisan election boards. Perhaps a sufficient explanation is incompetence, then, or mistakes? Maybe. Yet it doesn't escape notice that nearly every irregularity seemed to favor Bush votes over Kerry's. That pattern undermines the randomness one would normally expect from irregularities resulting from mistakes or incompetence.

On the other side, Republicans accused Democrats in Ohio of falsely registering voters. This was not a new charge, but in the 2004 election it acquired a new ferocity, fed by reports that Democratic-leaning Franklin County had voter registration numbers that exceeded the voting age population (but so did three heavily GOP counties, with 26 other counties, most of them GOP, having voter registration that exceeded an unlikely 90 percent of their populations).[10] Republicans brought to Ohio thousands of activists and lawyers to act as poll monitors who challenged the voter registration of primarily minority voters in heavily Democratic urban neighborhoods of Cleveland, Dayton, and other cities. The Democrats matched the Republican operatives person for person, turning the approach to the polls into a thuggish gauntlet that had the effect of slowing down the line.[11]

Florida did not escape scrutiny in 2004. In a partial replay of its 2000 debacle, when voter rolls were misused to purge thousands of qualified black voters by wrongly claiming they were convicted felons, another attempt was made to purge black voters from the voter rolls as being ex-felons. This time the operation was discovered and halted.[12] But other problems developed. In Broward County, a heavily Democratic region, 58,000 absentee ballots were not delivered on time within a few days of the election, and many of these voters were never able to vote.[13]

Problems developed in other battleground states as well. Minority and student voters in states such as New Mexico, Colorado, Minnesota, and Michigan experienced higher levels of voter intimidation and harassment than other groups, including being asked to show voter IDs though not required by law.[14] At least 1.2 million Americans voted incorrectly because of poor ballot design.[15] Not all the problems involved the presidential election. In Washington state, the governor's race required three recounts and was decided by 129 votes. After Republican gubernatorial candidate Dino Rossi claimed victory, a hand recount found more than 700 valid absentee ballots had been discarded because of inadequate procedures for verifying signatures. Even after Democrat Christine Gregoire was declared the victor, questions remained over possible ineligible voters casting ballots.[16]

In Ohio, all of these irregularities culminated in a recount of the ballots. One of the last lines of defenses against fraud, a recount tries to replicate the election results in a handful of randomly selected precincts. Yet problems developed there as well, leading to charges and lawsuits about the lack of statewide standards used for the recounts—the very reason cited by the U.S. Supreme Court for halting the Florida recounts in 2000 that elected Bush president. Perhaps most disturbing, in Hocking County, three days before the statewide recount was to begin, deputy elections director Sherole Eaton reported that an employee of the Triad company, which supplies voting equipment in 41 Ohio counties (and whose owner is a Republican donor),[17] came into her office to prepare for the recount, so that "the count would come out perfect and we wouldn't have to do a full hand recount of the county." He asked which precincts would be recounted, even though the selection of the precincts is supposed to be random. Working unsupervised, claiming to be repairing the main computer, he gained access to the central tabulator, which is the guts of the elections process where ballot records are stored and compiled. Voting machine experts cried foul, claiming this threatened the integrity of the recount in that county and perhaps others where Triad was the contractor. This prompted Congressman John Conyers (D-MI) to request an FBI investigation into illegal election tampering. Eaton suddenly found herself in a lot of hot water and backed off some of her claims. Later, she was fired.[18]

So who really won the 2004 election? The only honest answer is that we do not know for sure who won in Ohio—and hence the presidency. The evidence of electoral fraud is provocative and disturbing, and some of it inspires outrage, but there's no smoking gun. The National Research Commission on Elections and Voting, a panel formed in the aftermath of the 2004 election and composed of some the nation's top elections scholars, found no conclusive proof of a stolen election, but it concluded that there were "pervasive breakdowns in election administration and oversight" that "make it impossible to definitively put theories and accusations of fraud to rest." Moreover, the commission concluded that these ongoing problems threaten the integrity and credibility of America's electoral process.[19] In other words, for the second time we held an election for the most powerful elective office in the world, and we couldn't guarantee the integrity and security of the vote. All Americans of whatever political stripe should find that disturbing.

21

FAILED ELECTION ADMINISTRATION, COAST TO COAST

The day following Election 2004, retiring NBC News anchor Tom Brokaw told a national TV audience, "We've gotta fix the election system in this country." In an unusually serious interview with David Letterman, Brokaw called for stronger national standards in how we count the votes. What Brokaw and others have realized is that, more than voting snafus in any one or two states, the central problem is a failed election administration regime, coast to coast. Election management in the United States amounts to a decentralized hodgepodge of over 3,000 counties and 9,000 townships with few national standards to guide them. Some states establish their own statewide standards, but those standards are arbitrarily enforced and frequently seem to be playing catch-up to changes in technology for voting equipment. Voting systems consultant Erik Lazarus has made the staggering claim that the United States provides more security, testing, and oversight of slot machines and the gaming industry than of our nation's voting equipment or election administration.[20]

At the top of this failed administration heap are the secretaries of state who oversee elections in each of the 50 states. Ohio's secretary of state, Kenneth Blackwell, played the same conflicting role in the 2004 presidential election as notorious GOP secretary of state Katherine Harris in Florida in 2000. He seemed to do his best to disrupt any attempt at accountability. In the days leading up to the election, Blackwell sought to rule out largely Democratic voter registrations submitted on paper of the wrong weight, and to strictly limit the counting of provisional ballots (disproportionately used by minorities) to ones cast only in the correct precinct, which violated the spirit of the federal right to a provisional ballot. These decisions, combined with his lack of oversight of the recount, created ample controversy for those looking for a villain.

In fact, one of the most disturbing developments from the 2004 election was the fact that the secretaries of state overseeing elections in three battleground states—Ohio, Missouri, and Michigan—were cochairs of their state's George Bush reelection campaigns. It was as if Katherine Harris, who as Florida's secretary of state had served as the Bush campaign's cochair in the 2000 election, had cloned herself. In Missouri, the Republican secretary of state also was running for governor—he oversaw elections for his own race (which he won). But the Democrats weren't about to be outdone; in West Virginia, the Democratic secretary of state was overseeing elections in which *he* was running for governor (he won as well). In Florida, a highly partisan Republican secretary of state again oversaw the elections; and in New Mexico, another battleground state, a highly partisan Democrat was secretary of state making decisions that had Republicans crying foul. A political scientist from Mexico City monitoring the 2004 election told *Business Week* that election administration in the United States "looks an awful lot like the old Mexican PRI to me," referring to the notorious party that dominated Mexican politics for seven decades by rigging elections. American states have no reason, he stated, not to set up nonpartisan election commissions with citizen oversight.[21]

Following the Florida meltdown in 2000, the failings of the current administrative regime became more apparent over the issue of computerized voting, also known as touch screens or DREs (short for *direct recording equipment*). Respected computer experts have spread the alarm that a rogue programmer might be able to covertly instruct the voting computer to assign every fourth vote for a Democratic candidate to a Republican candidate, or vice versa. The distress has spread like wildfire, fueled by actual reports in the 2004 election from several states. In Florida and New Mexico, some voters using touch screens reported that their selection of John Kerry automatically turned into a vote for President Bush. In Broward County, Florida, software subtracted votes rather than added them. While these snafus were detected and corrected, it's the fear of the undetectable that drives a panicky reaction by computer scientists and concerned citizens. Many scenarios of electoral fraud amount to outlandish fantasies fit for a sci-fi thriller, with little basis in reality, but the lack of a voter-verified paper receipt—like we receive from ATM machines for our personal financial transactions—undermines public confidence in the ability to recount the ballots in a disputed election.

Feeding the public unease is the dubious behavior of the manufacturers and sellers of the voting equipment. The elections industry has been mired in controversy for quite some time. In the mid-1990s, the voting equipment industry was dominated by a single company, Business Records Corporation (BRC), an 800-pound gorilla that became the target of a little-publicized antitrust and antiracketeering lawsuit by the Department of Justice, resulting in the breakup of BRC. Today, the field is dominated by three companies: Elections Systems and Software (ES&S), Sequoia Voting Systems, and Diebold Election Systems. I've had various contacts with all three of these companies, and none of them inspires confidence. They are best described as relatively small, for-profit corporations that make their buck by too often cutting corners, fighting innovation, and producing equipment that isn't as good as it could or should be. These companies develop their own private software and hardware, which is then tested by ill-equipped federal laboratories and state authorities and sold to county administrators who are barely knowledgeable about technology or the vendors. Diebold and ES&S have been caught red handed inserting software patches into their computerized touch screen equipment that have not passed through required testing and certification procedures.

Cause for additional concern is the shoddy procedures used for testing and certifying voting equipment. The three federal testing laboratories—called "independent testing authorities," even though two of them, Ciber, Inc., and Wyle Laboratories, have donated tens of thousands of dollars to GOP candidates and the Republican National Committee[22]—test the software and hardware for voting equipment. Yet there is little federal oversight of these labs, which in any case are ill suited for the job. New voting technologies get in line behind toasters and refrigerators for testing. More cause for concern is that the shoddy certification procedures are greased by a revolving door between government regulators and the industry, as well as the usual corporate methods of influence peddling.

In California, where 58 counties are expected to buy about $400 million in new equipment by 2007, voting machine makers have hired former government officials to supply prestige for a competitive edge. Former GOP secretary of state Bill Jones, who was his state's chief regulator of the industry, became a paid consultant to Sequoia. Former GOP New Hampshire governor John Sununu has acted as a private consultant to contact customers on behalf of Diebold. Former secretaries of state from Florida and Georgia have signed on as lobbyists for ES&S and Diebold.[23] One vendor competing for $100 million in contracts treated Ohio election officials to free meals, limousine rides, and concert tickets. Other vendors have spent untold amounts on major conferences for election officials, footing the bill for hospitality suites, banquets, lobster bakes, and pool parties. There have been attempts to crack down on the revolving door and influence peddling, but the practices are still common.[24]

But perhaps most unsettling are the links discovered between the heads of the three largest corporations selling voting equipment and the upper echelons of the Republican Party. The executives and founders of the big three vendors are all big GOP donors, pouring hundreds of thousands of dollars into party coffers in the past few years. Walden O'Dell, Diebold's CEO, has been a Bush "pioneer" who attended strategy powwows at the president's Crawford, Texas, ranch and infamously wrote in a fund-raising letter that he was "committed to helping Ohio deliver its electoral votes to the president" even as his company was seeking multimillion-dollar contracts in Ohio for providing computerized voting equipment.[25] Chuck Hagel, former chairman of ES&S's parent company, left that position and was elected as a Republican senator from Nebraska less than eight months later, with his former company's machines counting the votes.[26] To illustrate the absurdity of this practice, federal law forbids your local postal clerk from working on federal election campaigns to prevent an army of federal employees from being ordered to assist the president's or congressperson's reelection. Yet no such firewall exists between political campaigns and the private corporations whose machines count our ballots, or between the secretaries of state or election administrators overseeing our elections.

Perhaps the biggest threat to our elections is that no one seems to be steering the ship. There is no central brain or team that has a handle on all aspects, developing best practices or a road map that states and counties can follow. This was painfully obvious when I attended the Voting Systems Testing Summit in November 2005, which marked the first time that representatives from all the different camps involved with or concerned about election administration—top federal regulators, vendors, testing laboratories, state and local election administrators, computer scientists, and public advocates—came together in one place. What was most striking was that, much like our broken decentralized health care system, no one could articulate a comprehensive inventory of the many problems, much less a blueprint for the solutions. Instead, there was a lot of finger pointing and excuses. Tragically, while Congress has appropriated $3 billion for buying new voting equipment, the money is arriving before the necessary standards and best practices are in place to ensure that the money isn't wasted. This hardly looks like the world's greatest democracy in action.

HOW TO SECURE THE VOTE

The 2004 election, on the heels of the 2000 election, serves as a dire warning that our ability to run free and fair elections is in danger. It's very much like the repeated warnings in New Orleans about the vulnerability of its levees. Without modernization of our administrative practices and equipment, as well as more government oversight and vigilance, our elections will remain vulnerable to breakdown and fraud. Here are the reforms necessary for modernizing our elections and making sure that every vote is counted.

Impartial election officials. At the top of the list must be creating a bureaucracy of impartial, nonpartisan election officials. We should have learned this lesson in the 2000 presidential election when Katherine Harris oversaw the Florida election as both secretary of state and cochair of George Bush's election committee. If it can't be guaranteed that the partisan loyalties of election managers will play no role in deciding outcomes, then elections become a charade. It hardly matters if the voting technology is paper ballots or computerized voting if the election administrators are partisan motivated or crooked; fraud with paper ballots has occurred throughout American history. Thus, election officials should be forbidden from serving as cochairs of campaigns, and clear regulations and ethical guidelines should restrict the involvement of election officials in political campaigns. To avoid even a question of bias, elections policies and procedures should be set well in advance of the election by a commission of officials who are nonpartisan or represent a wide spectrum of political beliefs.

Professionalization and training of election officials. In addition to nonpartisanship, election administration should be upgraded to that of a professional civil service position as a way of ensuring competence, training, and impartiality. Running elections has become increasingly complex, involving (especially in the larger jurisdictions) dozens of employees and thousands of volunteers, and requiring a sophisticated knowledge of software, databases, voting equipment, organizational management, and public relations. Yet there are no vocational schools or degree programs where one can learn how to administer such a highly complex process. It's all on-the-job training. The elections director of one large California county was an elections clerk answering telephones only a few years before becoming director; before that he wrote product descriptions for a seafood company. California's chief technical consultant has a background in aerospace engineering, not computerized voting equipment. Election administrators and technical consultants should be specially trained, professional civil servants who are tested for a demonstrated proficiency with using appropriate technology, running elections, and making the electoral process transparent and secure. Better training also should be extended to poll workers and the armies of volunteers needed to administer an election.

National elections commission. Most established democracies use national election commissions to establish nationwide standards and uniformity and to foster accountability. But in the United States, we leave election administration to thousands of local officials with little in the way of common standards or uniformity. Imagine if our railway lines, highways, or airline regulations had no national consistency, and so traveling from state to state was mired by confusion and varying quality. This crazy hodgepodge creates wide discrepancies from state to state and county to county in the testing and quality of voting equipment, recounts, poll worker training, the use of absentee and provisional ballots, and many other administrative details.

For example, a hand recount after the election of a number of randomly selected precincts is one of the best safeguards for detecting malfunctioning voting equipment or fraud. Yet there's no uniformity or standard for the number of ballots that need to be hand recounted to provide adequate security. Some states require that 5 percent of precincts must be hand recounted; other states require 4 percent; still others require only 1 percent, five times fewer than other states. Which number is the best practice? Nobody seems to know or is attempting to figure it out. This is a formula for unfair elections and electoral meltdowns. A centralized policymaking commission will benefit all voters. Just as the National Highway Board is empowered to set standards for highway design and construction, a national elections commission should have the authority to create minimum standards that states must follow to ensure the quality of elections. It's just common sense.

The U.S. Election Assistance Commission (EAC), established in the wake of the Florida debacle by the Help America Vote Act of 2002, represents the beginning of a national commission, but it needs to be strengthened greatly. A more robust EAC would partner with the states and counties to establish nationwide standards for high-quality elections. It also would oversee a rigorous federal testing and certification process for voting equipment and software, include random checks of voting equipment on election day (called "parallel monitoring").[27] A more robust commission also could provide more stringent oversight to the federal testing laboratories; develop open source software and government-owned "public interest" voting equipment (more on that later); assist states in developing their federally mandated statewide voter registration databases; and crack down on the revolving door between state election regulators and the voting equipment industry. A commission also should set uniform standards for provisional ballots, ballot design, poll worker training, polling place locations, and ballot access for presidential candidates. It could enforce laws prohibiting voter suppression and intimidation. It also should provide rigorous evaluation of what works and what can be improved, and develop and propagate the best practices.

Despite this urgent need, disappointingly, the National Association of Secretaries of State (NASS), the professional organization for all chief election officers, voted at its 2005 annual meeting that Congress should dissolve the EAC as an interference on states' rights. This decision reveals what an ossified mind-set prevails among many of our states' chief election officers. Apparently they want no oversight or regulation whatsoever over their dealings. But even more disturbing, the *New York Times* reported that 43 percent of the NASS budget comes from voting machine companies and other vendors.[28] Cronyism and ethical conflicts have crept like a weed into every crack and crevice of our election administration.

A "voter-verified paper trail."   If computerized voting equipment can be made secure, it offers several advantages over older technologies (including voting by paper, which some have nostalgically called for). For example, optical scan and computerized touch screen equipment offer "error notification," in which voters are automatically alerted to any mistakes they make on their ballot. As a step toward making this technology secure, fair elections advocates should demand a voter-verified paper trail so that any recounts can be conducted with a copy of the voter's ballot that has been self-verified. Not only is that approach a check for uncovering administration errors or fraud, but it also will help restore the confidence of the public. We have such an audit trail for ATM transactions, and our votes are no less important. Note that optical scan voting equipment, where voters make marks on their ballot with a pen (e.g., coloring in ovals, like on many standardized tests) automatically has a voter-verified paper trail—it's your ballot. But an auditable paper trail should be seen as a minimum. Without impartial election officials and a national commission establishing uniform standards, a voter-verified paper trail alone will not guarantee the integrity and security of our elections.

"Public interest" voting equipment. The Holy Grail of election administration practices is public interest voting equipment, where the states and/or the federal government develop their own voting equipment. Instead of the nuts and bolts of our democracy being in the hands of private companies, a government elections commission would contract with the sharpest minds in the private sector to develop open source software and off-the-shelf hardware that would be owned and managed by the state or federal government. That voting equipment then could be offered, either in competition with the private sector or solely as part of a statewide system deployed to rich and poor neighborhoods alike, to ensure that every voter is using the same, best equipment. Also, the testing and certification process would be fully public, subject to the rules and disclosures of open government, instead of how it is now, usually behind closed doors with little accountability.

Lest this suggestion seem radical, other nations such as Belgium, India, Argentina, and Brazil already do this. India, which is the world's largest democracy with twice as many voters as the United States, held nationwide elections with voters from New Delhi to the Himalayas, illiterate voters and polyglot communities, nearly all of them voting on the same computerized equipment owned, developed, and operated by the government in conjunction with the private sector.[29] It is hard for a nation as proud as the United States to admit that we are playing catch-up to India and Brazil when it comes to election administration, but that is in fact the case. This is not rocket science, yet the United States lags woefully behind. States could do this on their own and not wait for the federal government. Georgia already has a statewide system, and Brit Williams, who conducts Georgia's certification evaluations, says, "Having a statewide system allows every county, regardless of wealth, to have the same system which also helps the state give technical support and training to all those counties. Everybody learns the same thing, it's not a hodge-podge."[30]

Some of my recommendations can be enacted on the county or state levels (professional and nonpartisan election officials, auditable paper trails, and public interest voting equipment); the battle for a national elections commission and uniform standards must be fought at the federal and state levels. There is a need for a long-term commitment to funding our elections. The $3 billion provided by the Help America Vote Act (HAVA) for the purchase of new voting equipment was the first time the federal government has helped fund elections. Federal funding should be ongoing, not just a one-time fix, to help the states pay for voter databases, better training, and other critical needs besides equipment.

While reform efforts have a long way to go, certainly there are reasons for optimism. Various organizations (listed at the end of this chapter) have sprung up and are pressing for change, with degrees of success. Over half the states now require some kind of paper audit trail for their elections. The passage of the Help America Vote Act in 2002 showed that the Democratic Party sometimes can attract enough GOP votes in Congress to pass reform. In the wake of the problems revealed by the 2004 presidential election, a Commission on Federal Election Reform was established, cochaired by former president Jimmy Carter and former secretary of state James Baker. Baker's participation was particularly interesting since he had been George W. Bush's attorney in Florida who worked so hard to stop the recounting of ballots. The Carter-Baker Commission made several bold recommendations that earned bipartisan support, including nonpartisan election officials, a voter-verified paper trail, uniform standards for provisional ballots, universal voter registration, free media access for candidates, and more.[31]

Our poor performance in recent elections serves as a warning: Our antiquated electoral infrastructure and bureaucracy is inadequate for the 21st century. It's a wonder things run as well as they do. If we Americans cannot trust the integrity of our elections, whether because of incompetence, lousy technology, poor administration, or outright fraud, it will result in widespread apathy and resignation. Make no mistake about it—we are running our elections on borrowed time. Enacting the recommendations in this chapter will vastly improve election administration and secure the vote for the future.

▓ Summary of Recommendations

1. Impartial election officials
2. Professionalization of election administration
3. National elections commission
4. Require a voter-verified paper audit trail for voting equipment
5. "Public interest" voting equipment, designed and owned by the government, or at least a statewide uniform system of voting equipment
6. A long-term commitment and adequate funding of our elections

▓ Organizations to Contact

National Committee for Voting Integrity, **www.votingintegrity.org**, (202) 483-1140

Electionline.org, information clearinghouse, (202) 338-9860

Election Assistance Commission, **www.eac.gov**

California Voter Foundation, **www.calvoter.org**, (530) 750-7650

Black Box Voting, **www.blackboxvoting.org**

National Ballot Integrity Project, **www.ballotintegrity.org**

Verified Voting Foundation, **www.verifiedvoting.org**

2

Expand Voter Participation

The history of voting in the United States has been an epic jour-
ney, filled with heroism and tragedy. In his magisterial history,
*The Right to Vote: The Contested History of Democracy in the United
States*, Alex Keyssar shows that the struggle to extend the franchise to the poor, women, and slaves was hard-fought, with retreats
as well as advances. "Some Americans who had been enfranchised
in 1800 were barred from the polls by mid-century. Change was
neither linear nor uncontested," writes Keyssar.[1] He tracks the
ebbs and flows across the centuries, showing that political elites
shifted opinion, sometimes thinking of voting as a right, other
times as a privilege.

Truth be told, many of the Founding Fathers didn't give a fig
about the rights of the common citizen. In 1790, only a small
pool of perhaps 200,000 white males was eligible to vote, and owning property was a requirement of enfranchisement. The Founders
were nearly as fearful of Shay's Rebellion, an insurgency in 1786
of poor farmers and debtors in Massachusetts, as they were of
kingly despotism. John Jay, Founding Father, first chief justice,
and president of the First Continental Congress, expressed an
all-too-typical attitude shared by many of his colleagues (including James Madison in his early years and George Washington)
when he stated that the upper classes "were the better kind of
people, by which I mean the people who are orderly and industrious," and "the people who own the country ought to govern it."[2]

Two hundred years later, President Richard Nixon revealed
utter contempt for broad-based democracy when, in the confes-
sional of the Oval Office, he commented to John Erlichman:

You gotta remember, the smartest thing the [Founders] did was to limit the voters in this country. Out of 3.5 to 4 million people, 200,000 voted. And that was true for a helluva long time, and the republic would have never survived if all the dummies had voted along with the intelligent people. Now . . . you got people voting now—blacks, whites, Mexicans, and the rest—that shouldn't have anything to say about government; mainly because they don't have the brains to know.[3]

Unfortunately, that ugly attitude is still all-too-present today, incubating, awaiting its moment to crawl forth and reassert itself. We can recognize it when only racial minorities are asked to show identification before voting. We can see it when the new federal right to a provisional ballot is hamstrung in various states and counties by narrow interpretations that disenfranchise voters. We see it emerging in the callous way in which Motor Voter legislation, which requires social service agencies to offer voter registration to the poor, has been feebly implemented. We see it in the 50 to 60 million eligible voters who are unregistered, disproportionately minority, poor, and young. And we see it manifest in Florida when in 2000 election officials set up police roadblocks near some black polling stations, and in Georgia when the government passed a law making poor and elderly voters pay for a required voter ID, tantamount to a poll tax (later overturned by the courts).

It's ironic, but today our former European colonizers seem to be more committed to political pluralism and participation than we are. The United States could learn a lot by examining what other democracies do. Here are several important measures, already in use around the world, that would do a lot to fully enfranchise all Americans.

Universal voter registration. The United States is one of the few established democracies that does not practice "universal voter registration." With universal voter registration, everyone who is 18 years of age or older and eligible to vote *automatically* is registered to vote by the government. There are no forms to fill out, nothing the citizen need do. The government takes responsibility for registering all eligible voters. Iraq has a higher share of its adult citizens registered to vote than the United States because the Iraqi government assumed the responsibility of registering its voters. If we had universal voter registration, we would immediately add 50 million Americans to the voter rolls, nearly one in three eligible voters, disproportionately minority, poor, and young adults. Implemented fully, universal voter registration would be one of the most important civil rights accomplishments since the Voting Rights Act of 1965.

Not only does universal voter registration lead to more complete voter rolls, but it also results in less voter fraud. When the government takes a proactive, ongoing role, registration occurs in an orderly manner on a steady, rolling basis. But with our current practices, voter registration drives occur in spurts right before major elections and often are left up to partisan organizations. This approach invites electoral fraud because partisan organizations have incentive to try to manipulate the voter rolls, adding fictitious names, doubly registering its own voters, or suppressing the opposition's voters. In the 2004 election, we saw incidents where a Republican-linked voter registration firm in Nevada and Oregon was caught throwing out forms collected from voters registering as Democrats.[4] In cities such as Milwaukee and Chicago, Republicans accused Democratic urban machines of registering dead people to vote (though there is little evidence of that practice). The inevitable result of this kind of partisan registration process is that judges get involved in deciding close elections.

The lack of an orderly, rolling, automatic registration process also creates problems for election administrators. Major voter registration drives result in a surge of registrations right before an election that must be quickly processed. That likely was one of the reasons for the long lines at Ohio polling places. This scenario caught election officials completely unprepared without enough equipment or the ability to tell late-registering voters where to vote, which led to many voters using provisional ballots (with many of the provisional ballots never actually being counted). One-third of the over 400,000 phoned complaints received by toll-free hotlines on or before Election Day were the result of registration problems.[5]

Universal voter registration offers the promise of both *clean* and *complete* voter rolls. It is the best way to bring together conservatives concerned about fraud in elections and liberals concerned about low voter registration. With comprehensive databases and full registration, there is no longer a question about who is or is not registered—everyone is registered. It provides a coherent system that ensures all of us can vote, but none of us can vote more than once.

In the past, universal voter registration in the United States was technologically difficult, but that's no longer the case. As a result of the passage of the federal Help America Vote Act, which was enacted in the wake of the 2000 election meltdown, each state is mandated to create a statewide voter registration database. This database, if merged with each state's census database, Social Security database, driver's license database, and others, would enable universal registration. The creation of the database can be done on a state-by-state or a national basis. Both options have their pluses and minuses, but the basic goal does not change: automatic and universal voter registration of all eligible adults 18 years or older.

In the short term, other steps short of either a national database or statewide voter databases could bring us much closer to universal voter registration. We could expand Motor Voter, which now merely offers the option of registering to vote, so that all citizens applying for any state service *automatically* are registered to vote. We also could automatically register citizens who complete tax forms and any other state or federal applications. We could redesign post office change-of-address forms to double as voter registration forms. Or we could copy the successful practice used in the United Kingdom, which requires the government to send every residence a notice of those registered at that location. Residents may add to the form the names of unregistered eligible voters in their household and mail it back.

One promising possibility would be to focus on the population that typically has the lowest rates of registration: young adults. A state or county could have high schools preregister to vote all their students as they enter their junior year. These preregistrations would be entered into the voter database just like any other registration, coded so that the computerized database is instructed to activate that registration when these preregistrants turn 18. Each new registrant would receive a letter alerting them about their eligibility to vote, the date of the next election, and their responsibilities when changing addresses.

Preregistration of high school students not only would enroll far more young people in an orderly way but would provide a means to introduce more young people to the importance of civic engagement since a natural complement to this policy would be a "voter's ed" curriculum, just as many high schools have driver's ed. Over time, as all 18-year-olds were registered to vote, the United States would move much closer to 100 percent voter registration. Scaled-down versions of these programs have been implemented in California, where community colleges work with the secretary of state to register students as they register for classes. Legislators in Illinois and Rhode Island have introduced legislation for high school preregistration. The United States needs to move much more vigorously in this direction.

One method that has been promoted by good government groups is Election Day Registration (EDR). With EDR, an eligible voter can register right up to and on Election Day. Six states use this kind of "one-step voting": Idaho, Maine, Minnesota,

New Hampshire, Wisconsin, and Wyoming. On average, these states have higher voter turnout than the rest of the nation, but it's not clear that EDR is the decisive factor, because these states also tend to be ones that exhibit more of Robert Putnam–like "social capital," which is correlated with higher voter turnout.[6]

EDR has many positives, but it still leaves the act of registering up to the individual, rather than making it a government function. And it requires more poll workers on Election Day to assist with registration, which could strain resources since finding poll workers in the middle of a busy workday has been increasingly difficult. EDR also has encountered opposition from election administrators who fear chaos on Election Day, as well as from conservatives who imagine busloads of voters fraudulently voting again and again in different precincts (though none of these nightmare scenarios has occurred in the six states that use EDR). Despite these objections, Election Day Registration is a good first step toward universal voter registration.

All of these practices would be better than what we do now. Unfortunately, fair-minded attempts to extend the franchise too often have been snagged in the partisan war. Because it is believed that minorities, young people, and the poor tend to vote more for Democrats, it has been difficult to build bipartisan consensus over proposals for expanding the franchise. The partisans don't care about what is right for our country, only how to seal their next victory.

Make voting easier: Election Day on a weekend or national holiday. Most modern democracies today vote on a holiday, a weekend, or over a series of days.[7] There is nothing sacred or even constitutional about voting on the first Tuesday in November, and most people have no recollection why President James Polk established the practice in 1845. Polk set the day after the fall harvest, allowing Monday as a travel day so that farmers could cast their ballots on Tuesday. A century and half later, most people don't live on farms, and Tuesday is a busy workday. A trip to the polls has become just another errand to squeeze around jobs, children, travel, and other responsibilities.

Voting on either a weekend or a holiday would promote the importance of American democracy and elections. Currently, the United States recognizes 10 federal holidays and a variety of state holidays, including Leif Eriksson Day (Minnesota), Columbus Day, Pioneer Day (Utah), Confederate Heroes Day (Texas), and Bird Day (Oklahoma). You'd think American democracy, one of the foundations of our national heritage, would rate at least as much recognition and celebration. A commission established in the wake of the 2000 meltdown, cochaired by former presidents Jimmy Carter and Gerald Ford, recommended that Election Day be a holiday. Yet even such a commonsense initiative met with ridiculously stubborn resistance from Congress. Recently, Senators John Kerry and Hillary Clinton introduced legislation to make Election Day a holiday.[8]

But states and local governments need not wait for the feds. In odd-numbered years, when only local races are on the ballot, local jurisdictions can hold elections on a weekend if they choose. And in nonpresidential election years, state elections for governor and other state offices can do the same or even make Election Day a state holiday. Some employers allow workers to take a half-day off on Election Day for the purposes of voting. Local and state authorities should move forward with these proposals and not wait for the federal government.

Make voting a right. The right to vote and the right to cast a free and secret ballot should be the foundation of democracy. Yet, as American voters discovered in 2000, we have no legal right to vote for president. In the Supreme Court decision that decided the presidential election, *Bush v. Gore*, the High Court reaffirmed that, under the U.S. Constitution, voting for president is reserved for state legislatures, which decide whether they wish to delegate it to the voters. Among the 120 or so nations with democratically elected governments, the United States is one of only 11 that doesn't grant its citizens an explicit constitutional right to vote.[9] Ironically, the new constitutions of Afghanistan and Iraq do grant this right to their citizens.

Increasingly, U.S. experts and democracy advocates believe that a solid legal foundation protecting an affirmative right to vote for every U.S. citizen is the key for enacting other political reforms. A right-to-vote constitutional amendment not only would guarantee the right of every citizen 18 and over to vote but also would empower Congress to set minimum national standards for all states to follow, provide protection against attempts to disenfranchise individual voters, and ensure that every vote cast is counted correctly. It would provide a vigilant guard against practices that can disenfranchise entire groups of voters such as minorities, felons, District of Columbia voters, and those using provisional ballots. Congressman Jesse Jackson Jr. from Illinois has introduced a constitutional amendment, House Joint Resolution 28, the Right to Vote Amendment. It has been cosponsored by more than 50 members of the House, though all are Democrats with one Independent. It likely has many years to go until enactment, but it's the right thing to do, and Americans who care about fair elections should support it.

Voting rights for Washington, D.C., residents. Most Americans assume that all U.S. citizens have a right to vote and a right to representation in the United States Congress. However, this is not the case. For the residents of Washington, D.C., Congress decides who may vote and for what office. Until 1961, D.C. residents did not have the right to vote for president, prompting the passage of the Twenty-third Amendment to the U.S. Constitution. Even today, more than a half million citizens living in our nation's capital have no voting representative in Congress. They pay federal taxes and can be drafted into the military, but they do not have representation in the U.S. Senate and elect only a non-voting delegate to the U.S. House of Representatives. As a result, D.C. residents are second-class citizens.

Ironically, D.C. residents did have representation in the early 1790s, but they lost their right to vote in 1801 when Congress voted to take control of the District of Columbia. This decision occurred a mere 26 years after the American patriots' famous declaration "No taxation without representation"—a motto that is emblazoned across all D.C. license plates today.[10]

Lack of D.C. voting rights costs us in international prestige. For example, when Representative Tom Davis (R-VA) participated in a delegation that was pressing Hong Kong leaders to allow democracy, a senior official responded, "Give your nation's capital the right to vote and then come talk to us about democracy."[11]

Congress should reinstate D.C. voting rights, and there are signs of bipartisan efforts to do that. In May 2005, Representative Davis introduced legislation to give D.C. a voting member in the House. Another bill introduced by Senator Joe Lieberman, the No Taxation without Representation Act, sought to give D.C. full congressional voting representation, including two senators.

Ex-felon and prisoner enfranchisement. The right to vote and to cast a free and secret ballot is supposed to be a cornerstone of democracy. Yet, upward of 4.7 million Americans will never be able to vote because of a felony incarceration on their record. In typically chaotic American fashion, different states treat felons differently. Only two states, Maine and Vermont, allow prisoners in jail to vote. Most states allow felons to vote after they have served their time, but many have created Byzantine procedures for restoring the individual's right to vote.[12] Some states, including Florida, Virginia, Texas, and Alabama, permanently ban felons from voting, even after they have served their time. This regulation has disproportionately impacted minority communities, which have higher rates of incarceration.[13]

Today's laws restricting prisoner voting rights are rooted in racism, dating to the Reconstruction era and the legacy of discriminatory Jim Crow laws. Over the last few years, advocates of restoring felon voting rights have successfully dismantled some of these laws. In 2005, Iowa and Nebraska passed legislation to reverse legacies of felony disenfranchisement.[14] But for every step forward there is a half step back. As we saw in Florida's 2000 election, felony voting lists were misused to disenfranchise thousands of African American voters who were not themselves ex-felons but who had names similar to an ex-felon's. The elections chief of one Florida county found her own name on her county's felon list!

This crazy hodgepodge of practices should be replaced by one national law. At the very least, those who have finished their jail time should be reenfranchised automatically via a simple and straightforward procedure. But one has to ask, What is the point of disenfranchising prisoners while serving time in jail? Many prisoners come from the poorest and most vulnerable communities, and while they are in jail is a good time to instill in them the good habits of citizenship, including voting. Like Maine and Vermont, most European democracies allow prisoners to vote because voting is considered a human right. In October 2005, the European Court of Human Rights struck down Britain's ban of prisoners voting, ruling, "[The] removal of the vote . . . runs counter to the rehabilitation of the offender as a law-abiding member of the community."[15] Ironically, Saddam Hussein, who was jailed and facing trial for mass murder, was permitted along with other prisoners by the Iraqi government and American military to vote in the December 2005 parliamentary elections.

But, like so much in American politics, the issue of felony enfranchisement gets snared in the partisan war. Because felons are disproportionately minority, and minorities vote overwhelmingly Democratic, Republicans generally are opposed to reinstatement of voting rights. Unfortunately, fairness, equality, and what's good for our country take a backseat to winning elections.

Prohibit voter suppression and intimidation. In a throwback to uglier times we thought we had put behind us, voter intimidation and suppression, especially of minority voters, have reappeared in some states. Numerous anecdotes have been reported of tactics designed to confuse and scare away voters. For example, in the 2004 election, flyers reportedly were distributed listing the wrong day for the election or saying Republicans should vote on Tuesday and Democrats should vote on Wednesday. Voters were told that traffic violations made it illegal for them to vote and that all parking tickets and overdue rent had to be paid before voting. Voters received mailings claiming that anyone registered by the National Association for the Advancement of Colored People (NAACP) was not allowed to vote. In its most flagrant forms, heavy police presence in minority precincts has been viewed as intimidating.

The Justice Department and state law enforcement officials must make monitoring and defending the right to vote a top priority. Election officials should allow international and nonpartisan election observers to observe polling places. Senator Barack Obama (D-IL) has introduced a bill, the Deceptive Practices and Voter Intimidation Prevention Act, that would create a criminal penalty for deceptive or intimidating practices. Such federal monitoring and intervention where necessary should be a priority.

Overseas voter enfranchisement. Americans living abroad face unique challenges when trying to vote. Voter registration is conducted through the Department of Defense (DOD), and the cumbersome procedure almost seems designed to fail unless you are connected to the military bureaucracy. Between three and seven million U.S. citizens live abroad at any one time (although the number is inexact, and no particular governmental agency or researcher seems to have a handle on this figure). I have met many expatriates with horror stories about attempts to register and vote—forms lost or misplaced, rude bureaucrats, and American embassies that were politely or rudely inept. While much effort is made to register military voters and deliver their absentee ballots, in many cases even soldiers' registrations have not been processed, or the absentee ballots arrived late or didn't arrive at all. This situation is particularly vexing with our men and women in uniform, who have enlisted to protect American freedom and security.

But the bureaucratic red tape frustrating military voters is nothing compared to that experienced by American civilians living abroad. I heard firsthand the frustration when I was on a lecture tour in Europe in May 2004, as overseas voters were gearing up for the presidential election. These Americans received practically no organized level of support when registering to vote or trying to procure their ballot. To vote, first they had to apply for a ballot to the Department of Defense. When the DOD ran out of applications, it created panic. Complicating all of this, as usual, was a subtext of partisan implications: For the 2004 election, it was widely believed that the military vote was mostly a Republican vote, while the nonmilitary vote was strongly Democrat. So when the DOD suddenly ran out of applications for nonmilitary expatriates, this situation immediately aroused suspicions. After many frantic phone calls to American embassies all over the world, more applications were obtained.

Once prospective voters receive their application from the DOD, they must mail it back to their local election official. But some states and counties seem unclear about their own procedures. Sometimes a state rejects the application of an expatriate for unknown reasons, or does not deal with it in a prompt fashion—and doesn't bother informing the voter. Plus, overseas voters must rely on mail traveling long distances, and the entire process can take quite a long time, with numerous points for failure. Other nations allow their overseas citizens to vote, but the procedure does not seem to be accompanied by the level of chaos and partisanship that afflicted our overseas vote in the 2004 election. This is yet another example of how Americans' inattention to detail has turned what should be a relatively simple and straightforward matter into a nightmare.

As in the other examples in this chapter, what seems apparent is how little Americans are willing to adapt and evolve—and how often partisan calculations obstruct enactment of the fairest and most commonsense changes. Americans assume that our voting institutions and practices are the best, but our blind spots and prejudices continue to hamper our elections. In too many ways, American democracy has become a museum rather than a living, breathing creation.

■ **Summary of recommendations:**

1. Universal voter registration
2. National voting holiday or weekend voting
3. "Right to vote" constitutional amendment
4. Washington, D.C., voting rights
5. Ex-felon and prisoner enfranchisement
6. Prohibition of voter suppression and intimidation
7. Overseas voter enfranchisement
8. International and nonpartisan election observers monitoring polling places

■ **Summary of recommendations:**

Demos, **www.demos-usa.org**, (212) 633-1405

FairVote, **www.fairvote.org**, (301) 270-4616

DC Vote, **www.dcvote.org**, (202) 462-6000

Right to Vote, Campaign to End Felony Disenfranchisement, **www.righttovote.org**

U.S. Commission on Civil Rights, **www.usccr.gov**

Democrats Abroad, **www.democratsabroad.org**

Republicans Abroad, **www.republicansabroad.org**

3

Increase Voter Choice with Instant Runoff Voting

I remember the night of March 2, 2002, like it was yesterday. We had fought a hard campaign to pass a political reform, known as Proposition A in San Francisco. I had led a merry band of idealistic election reformers who dared to believe we could convince an entire city that a new way of voting was the wave of the future.

Our opponents, mostly the usual mix of political consultants and downtown business interests who oppose change, had spent gobs of money to kill Proposition A. They mailed tens of thousands of citywide mailers slandering our efforts. They were willing to do and say anything to stop reform. As the polls closed on Election Night, I was exhausted. I had been awake for nearly 48 hours at that point, directing the troops, giving media interviews, and urging on my team of precinct walkers, street sign holders, phone bankers, and more. I remember scanning my to-do list, looking for the next task, unable to stop my campaign fervor. My co–campaign manager and fellow conspirator from the Center for Voting and Democracy, Caleb Kleppner, looked at me and said, "What are you doing? The polls have closed. We're finished. The election's over." I realized he was right. There was nothing left to do except wait for the results.

I slid into a chair with a sinking feeling. Our prospects for success suddenly looked grim. We were trying to pass a reform in San Francisco known as instant runoff voting, or IRV, which is an advanced method of voting that allows voters to rank their candidates, first choice, second choice, and third choice. If your first choice doesn't win, your vote goes to your second choice—that's your runoff choice, the candidate you prefer if your favorite candidate can't win. The goal is to elect candidates who have support from more than 50 percent of voters and get it over in one election. Voters are liberated to vote for the candidates they really like instead of choosing the "lesser of two evils" or having to worry about spoiler candidates messing up the results.

In effect, IRV asks the voters to tell us more about themselves. OK, you know who your favorite candidate is, but tell us more—tell us who your second-favorite is in case your first choice can't win. OK, you're a moderate Democrat, but what about this moderate Republican candidate? Might that candidate be acceptable as your second or third choice? Or maybe you are a Libertarian Party supporter, or a Green Party supporter—tell us who your second or third choice candidates might be in case your Libertarian or Green candidate can't win. Voters can think more about which candidates they like regardless of partisan labels. And this in turn fires the synapses of voters in ways that the current system can never do.

With IRV, for example, the nearly 100,000 Ralph Nader voters in Florida during the 2000 presidential election would have had the option of ranking a second choice. No question, thousands of them would have ranked Al Gore, who would have been the recipient of all those runoff votes, winning Florida and the presidency. History would have been changed. Likewise, in the 1992 presidential election, the first President Bush could have won second choices from Ross Perot voters, and he might have beaten Bill Clinton, who won the presidency with only 43 percent of the national popular vote. So instant runoff voting can change outcomes and produce fairer results. And IRV leads to a more satisfactory experience in the voting booth because suddenly voters aren't trapped in the dilemma of always picking the lesser of two evils. You can cast your vote for your favorite candidate, knowing that if your favorite can't win, you can give your vote to your second choice.

Waiting for the initial results that election night, I reflected on the fact that no ranked ballot system like IRV had been enacted in the United States in 40 years. Americans are used to thinking that we are the paragon of democracy, that the way we elect our representatives is the best—indeed, the only way. Most Americans, even many political scientists, are not aware of the vast array of electoral methods available and used in other nations, almost all of them better than the methods we currently use. With that kind of hubris, it's no wonder we had an electoral meltdown in the 2000 presidential election. And it makes many Americans very close-minded about trying other methods. I was quite familiar with the overwhelming tide of inertia that political reformers face in the United States. Yet against all those odds and more, we in San Francisco had been audacious enough to believe that we could convince an entire city to take a chance on an advanced method such as instant runoff voting. Such hopeless dreamers!

I got up from my chair to look at the television monitor where the first election returns would soon appear. In San Francisco, the first returns come from the early batch of absentee voters, a sizable number who returned their ballots in the days and weeks before Election Day. For various reasons, these voters tend to be more conservative and dislike change, so we didn't have terribly high hopes of doing well with them. We had mailed some campaign flyers to them, and used automated robocalls, too, and I had calculated that if we could win approximately 45 percent of the votes from these absentee voters, that outcome would put us in very good shape for a possible victory. But if we won 40 percent or less from these early absentees, our hopes probably would be sunk. As I scanned the monitors, that's the amount I was hoping for.

The first figures came across the screen a few minutes later. My eyes were bleary, my eyeglass lenses filthy. I had to clean them and look again. And then my heart sank. On the screen I saw 39 percent. My disappointment sank to the pit of my stomach and into my feet. We had lost the election, I was sure of it.

But to my surprise I heard a roar of jubilation arising from the gathering postelection crowd in the next room. They also were watching the election returns on computer monitors. Caleb came rushing into the room—"Can you believe it? Fifty-nine percent from early absentees! Fifty-nine percent!"

I did a double take. I wiped off my glasses and looked again. I had misread it—59 percent, not 39! Instantly the telephones began ringing. The media wanted some quotes from me; they had all but declared victory for us. I'm cautious when it comes to electoral campaigns, so I was not ready to declare victory. I mumbled the usual prudent things, such as "We are cautiously optimistic . . . we are very gratified by the early returns," and so on. But everyone knew what it meant. Victory was ours. And I was growing excited despite my overwhelming fatigue. We had managed to pass one of the most significant electoral reforms in decades.

San Francisco held its first IRV election in November 2004. It was a momentous occasion because it showed that significant political reform was possible. Other cities and counties in the United States also have passed ballot measures for instant runoff voting. Bills have been introduced into state legislatures in more than 20 states. Support has been gained from the left and the right, from John McCain to Howard Dean. And it's the right kind of reform for our country at this time. When asked whether our nation should do away with the existing two-party system, a clear majority of Americans say yes. Yet our 18th-century electoral methods create and reinforce the two-party system. More modern methods such as instant runoff voting and others are better suited for our 21st-century politics.

HOW IRV WORKS

Instant runoff voting simulates a series of runoff elections to produce a majority winner in a single election. At the polls, voters pick their favorite candidate, but they also may indicate their second (i.e., runoff) choice, and even another runoff choice, ranking them on their ballots as 1, 2, and 3. After the polls close, the ballots are counted in the following way.

First, only the number one rankings on each ballot are counted. If a candidate receives a majority of first rankings, she wins, which is exactly the way we do it now. But if no candidate wins a majority of first rankings, then the "instant runoff" begins. The candidate with the fewest first rankings is eliminated, and a runoff round of counting occurs immediately. In this round each voter's ballot counts for your top-ranked candidate still in the race. For supporters of the eliminated candidate, your ballot counts for your second choice; this is your runoff choice that you would support if forced to come back to the polls for a two-round runoff. All the ballots are retallied, and if any candidate now has an overall majority of ballots (which now includes voters' first rankings but also the second rankings—i.e., runoff choices—from voters of any eliminated candidates), that candidate is declared the winner. If not, we eliminate the next candidate with the least number of votes and redistribute the runoff votes. Rounds of counting continue like this until there is a majority winner.

In other words, voters are ranking their runoff choices at the same time as their first choice, and these runoff rankings are used to determine which candidate has support from a popular majority. Voters are suddenly empowered to vote for the candidates we really like instead of being forced to pick between the lesser of two evils or a so-called spoiler.

THE CASE FOR IRV

There are many good reasons for using instant runoff voting, but a half dozen are especially important. I'll take these one at a time.

Elect majority winners. Three is a crowd in our current electoral system. Our plurality election process, where the highest vote getter wins even if less than a popular majority, breaks down when more than two candidates seek one office. In a three-way race, a candidate with only 37 percent of the vote can win the election, even though 63 percent of the voters wanted a different candidate. And this is not a mere theoretical consideration. In three of our last four presidential elections, the winning candidate did not have over 50 percent—a majority—of the national popular vote. Since 2000, governors in 15 states have won without a popular majority, including the last two California governors. In Massachusetts, the Democratic primary for governor was won by a candidate with a mere third of the vote. Jesse Ventura was elected governor of Minnesota as an independent, beating the Democratic and Republican candidates, with support from only 37 percent of voters. But with IRV, multiple candidates can run and not worry about the split votes that lead to nonmajority winners. With IRV, majority winners are elected in a single race.

No more spoiler dilemmas.   Our "plurality wins all" electoral system has made politics vulnerable to spoiler candidacies where like-minded voters supporting different candidates run the risk of splitting their vote and helping elect the candidate they like the least. Recall the bitter accusations between the Nader and Gore camps as fears of spoiling—very realistic fears, it turned out—drove the candidates and their supporters further apart, rather than closer together. Similar tensions arose between Perot and Bush voters in 1992. Ironically, our current system causes candidates who have the *most* in common to rage against each other even more than against their ideological opposite. But with IRV, voters are liberated to vote for the candidates they really like without worrying about spoilers and wasting their vote. Like-minded candidates from different parties can form coalitions, either conscious or implied.

Increase political debate.   The spoiler dynamic suppresses new candidates and their ideas, which in turn suppresses political debate of the important issues facing our nation. Third parties and independent candidates often have played an important role in the American political system as the "laboratories for new ideas." Third parties and independents first proposed the abolition of slavery (Free Soil Party), prohibition (Prohibition Party), the income tax (Populist Party), social welfare programs (Socialist Party), the New Deal coalition (Progressive Party), and balanced budgets (Reform Party).[1] Other ideas advanced or helped along by third party efforts include women's suffrage, the 40-hour workweek, the end of child labor, Social Security, food and drug safety laws, workers' compensation, unemployment insurance, public education, public libraries, direct election of U.S. senators, and government regulation of monopolies.

The importance of third parties and independent candidacies is that they introduce not only new types of ideas and issues but also a new type of candidate who speaks directly to various constituencies and mobilizes them with a personal touch that only an authentic candidate can provide. Ross Perot, during his two candidacies in 1992 and 1996, gave voice to the frustrations of middle America stuck with budget deficits, an indifferent two-party tango, and a desire to "toss the bums out." Ralph Nader's candidacies in 2000 and 2004 became a vehicle for many younger people tired of politics as usual, as well as for labor unionists and others concerned about globalization, allowing them to support a candidate they believed in. IRV opens up the system and liberates voters to support these sorts of candidates—and their ideas—without the unintended consequences of spoiling. If their first choice can't win, their vote can go to a front-running candidate as their second or third choice. That in turn increases the debate of political ideas, which would be good for America.

Diminished campaign mudslinging. IRV also decreases some of the worst negative campaigning that has become a permanent feature of American political campaigns. That's because in traditional winner-take-all elections, if you and I are running against each other, head-to-head, I win as easily by driving voters away from you as by attracting them to me. The last candidate standing wins. So the optimal campaign strategy becomes attacking you and taking as few stands on issues as possible to avoid alienating a potential bloc of voters. This process is greatly augmented by the use of campaign technologies such as polling and focus groups to figure out what sound bites will effectively attack your opponent, as well as what careful positions to take on the leading issues. Unsurprisingly, our elections are lacking in substance and alienating to many.

In contrast, instant runoff voting discourages negative campaigning. Winners may need to attract the second or third rankings from the supporters of rival candidates, so candidates must be more careful about what they say about each other. The incentives are to find common ground and build coalitions with other candidates, rather than tearing each other down. During San Francisco's first use of IRV for local races, a *New York Times* headline read, "New Runoff System in San Francisco Has the Rival Candidates Cooperating." Observers long used to the blood sport of San Francisco politics were amazed to see some candidates forming electoral coalitions, downplaying negative attacks, even urging their supporters to rank a like-minded opponent as their second choice. That's because they knew the winner would need the second or third ranking from the supporters of losing candidates. For those tired of polarized politics and mudslinging campaigns, IRV has much to offer.

Decreased polarization in party primaries. Voter turnout in party primaries usually is very low, which serves to empower the extremes in each party and grant them influence greater than their actual numbers. In that electoral situation, extreme candidates can rely on their narrow core of voters to win their party's nomination, as the more moderate candidates split the rest of the vote. This dynamic makes it more difficult for candidates with politically moderate leanings to win primary elections and be considered for the general election. Because moderate politicians play a crucial role as legislative bridge builders, their absence leads to a more polarized government. So using IRV for primary elections would help break the stranglehold that partisan voters now have on the primary process. Instead of a November election dominated by the most partisan Democrats and Republicans, voters would see more independent and moderate candidates more to their liking that had not been eliminated during the primary.

In fact, using IRV, we could get rid of low-turnout party primaries altogether. We could re-create a version of the popular open ("blanket") primary that was lost in California and other states due to an adverse Supreme Court ruling. We could simply use IRV in a single November election to elect majority winners, saving taxpayers hundreds of millions of dollars currently spent to administer these unnecessary primary elections, and significantly expand voter choice and political debate. The political parties would pay for their own nominating procedure, either a primary or a caucus—saving taxpayers millions of dollars—and deliver as many or as few candidates as they wished to the November election. Voters would rank their favorite candidates from the multicandidate field, mixing and matching from all political parties. IRV would ensure that the winner has a majority of the popular vote, and the open primary format would give voters greater choice and foster a competitive environment bursting with political debate.

IRV is a nonpartisan reform, neither left nor right, that makes our elections more democratic and more efficient. In Utah, the Republican Party has used IRV to nominate its candidates for Congress and governor to ensure their nominees have support from a majority of Republican voters. In Louisiana, IRV is used for overseas voters because Louisiana has a two-round runoff system and has no time to mail a second ballot to overseas voters between the first and second rounds. So Louisiana mails one ballot initially and has those voters rank their runoff choices at the same time as their first choice. Arkansas recently began using IRV for its overseas military voters. IRV also is used to elect the president of Ireland, the mayor of London, and Australia's national House of Representatives.

CRITICISMS OF IRV

The primary criticism of instant runoff voting is that it's too complicated. But ranked ballot elections have been used all over the world, including in the United States, for nearly a century, and there's no evidence that voters have difficulty with ranking candidates. In fact, children in Ireland and Australia use this method to elect their school governments. So did high school students in San Francisco in 2004, nearly 8,000 voters, who elected a nonvoting student representative to the school board of education. I have given numerous demonstrations in homes for the elderly, and seniors quickly grasp how to rank their candidates. That's because ranking is something we do all the time, whether for our favorite flavors of ice cream, movies, or sports polls.

During San Francisco's first IRV election in November 2004, an exit poll conducted by the Public Research Institute at San Francisco State University found that 87 percent of voters said they understood how IRV works. The high level of understanding included all racial and ethnic groups, particularly Asians and Chinese-speaking language minorities. Only 13 percent of Asians and 12 percent of whites reported a lack of understanding of IRV, 12 percent of English speakers and 15 percent of Chinese speakers, and 20 percent of Latinos and 23 percent of African Americans. Another exit poll conducted by the Chinese American Voters Education Committee showed similar results. The San Francisco State report concluded, "The majority of voters knew about [instant runoff voting], understood it, and used it to rank their preferences. Further, after having used it most say they prefer it to the former runoff system."[2]

Thus, the argument that IRV is too complicated has little merit. Certainly voter education must accompany any change like this to the electoral system, but decades of experience shows that voters handle ranked ballots with great ease.

HOW DO WE ADVANCE IRV?

One of the nice things about instant runoff voting is that it can be used in all sorts of circumstances, not just public elections. I recall being in a tavern in Portland, Oregon, after I spoke at a conference, and the tavern had over a dozen microbrews. My table of six people wanted to order one pitcher of beer, so we ranked our favorites on a napkin and tallied the ballots in about 45 seconds. An amber ale won, as I recall, and a new audience was introduced to the wonders of ranked ballots.

Selecting your favorite food, beverage, or movie is a terrific way to introduce newcomers to IRV. But IRV has many other great applications. For instance, private organizations can use IRV to elect its officers. Just have your members rank their candidates on a paper ballot and count the ballots by hand. I have counted ballots for internal elections of numerous organizations, some with over a hundred voters, and it takes no more than 15 to 20 minutes to count the ballots and announce the winners. IRV also should be used in organizations to endorse candidates or ballot measures.

It also can be used in nongovernmental elections. For instance, the International Olympic Committee used a form of IRV to choose its 2012 host city for the XXX Olympiad. The runoff system was a key factor in London's getting the nod because it received only a quarter of the votes on the first counting. In later rounds the city picked up a number of second and third choices from the eliminated cities of New York, Moscow, and Madrid.

Ranked ballot methods already are used to elect student governments at many universities, including Harvard, Stanford, Duke, MIT, Princeton, UCLA, UC-Berkeley, and many others.

The Academy Awards uses a ranked ballot method to nominate the finalists in all the major categories for the Oscars. The American Political Science Association uses IRV to elect its president (and that group knows a thing or two about elections). The largest accounting firm in the world, PricewaterhouseCoopers, uses a ranked ballot method to elect its international board of directors.

In fact, it's not just public elections where we get into trouble when we don't use IRV. America Online recently sponsored an online poll to select the greatest American of all time. That's a pretty lofty claim, so you would want the winner to have clear support. Unfortunately, AOL used a plurality voting system, and the results shed little light on Americans' true choice. Ronald Reagan came in first with a mere 24 percent of the vote. Abraham Lincoln was very close behind with 23.56 percent. Martin Luther King Jr. won 19.7 percent, George Washington received 17.7 percent, and Benjamin Franklin won 14.9 percent of the vote. Because Reagan was chosen by such a slim margin in a highly fractured field of candidates, he may not have reflected the choices of the majority. In fact, 76 percent of voters chose another candidate. If AOL had used IRV and allowed voters to rank as many candidates as they wished, it would have produced a consensus candidate with majority support.[3]

Online polls are a particularly good venue for using IRV since the Web user interface is so easily adapted for an online ranked ballot. Voters can rank their choices, and the results are easily tabulated. Prior to San Francisco's first election using IRV, the organization DemoChoice created an online poll so that voters could vote for their candidates in an informal version of the real election well in advance of November. Thousands of voters did so, and the online races became so heated that the candidates began telling their supporters to go vote in the preelection.

Another good use of IRV is for filling vacancies through special elections. With the death in 2005 of longtime congressman Bob Matsui, California had to hold a special election. Special elections are notorious for low voter turnout, and by law, if no candidate wins a majority in a congressional special election, a second (runoff) election is required to fill the vacancy—an additional expense for taxpayers. If you don't hold a runoff election, then you risk the problem that occurred in Oakland, California, which held a special election to fill a city council vacancy only to see the winner take office with a mere 29 percent of the vote. So IRV provides a solution by electing majority winners in a single election.

One of the best uses for IRV is in local races. For instance, the city of Albuquerque, New Mexico, has had several mayors elected in recent years with about 30 percent of the vote. In New York's 2005 mayoral election, a close result in the Democratic primary meant the city had to waste millions of dollars preparing for a runoff it ultimately did not need when the front-runner clinched the nomination by 720 votes. In both cities, IRV would ensure the election of majority winners in a single election. Other cities or states electing leaders in multiple elections (including a primary-general election cycle) could see similar gains by adopting IRV.

Another prime candidate is Los Angeles, where the last two mayoral runoffs have been bruising slugfests between the same two candidates, James Hahn and Antonio Villaraigosa. Instead of hearing what's best for the city, voters heard what was worst about the future mayor of L.A. But Los Angeles could simply eliminate the runoff and use IRV to elect the winner in one election. With IRV, the four main candidates, Hahn, Villaraigosa, Bob Hertzberg, and Bernard Parks, would have been courting each other's supporters, trying to build coalitions, instead of attacking each other. Even the two front-runners would have laid off the worst attacks for fear of a backlash. This would have made campaign debate about the city's future more substantive.

It is important to note that instant runoff voting is a majoritarian system, and it is best to use it for executive races such as mayor, governor, and president rather than legislatures (for legislative races, a proportional representation system is superior to IRV—that's the subject of the next chapter). But using IRV would inject fresh candidates and new ideas into our moldy politics. And it would expand voter choice and allow more voters to feel like their votes counted for something, instead of feeling like they waste their votes on candidates who either have no chance of winning or are the lesser of two evils. Because of how ranked ballots use each voter's preferences so efficiently, some have called it "state-of-the-art" democracy. Certainly we could use more state-of-the-art democracy in the United States today.

■ Summary of Recommendations

1. Use instant runoff voting to elect all single-winner races at local, state, and federal levels, especially executive races such as mayor, governor, and president.
2. Use IRV to replace two-round runoff elections; for partisan primaries; to fill vacancies; for overseas voters in states with runoff elections; for ballot measures with a range of policy options.
3. For nongovernmental elections, use IRV to elect your organization's officers; to endorse candidates or ballot measures; for student government (high school or university); for online polls; for selecting your favorite food, beverage, or movie.

■ Organizations to Contact

FairVote, **www.fairvote.org**, (301) 270-4616

New America Foundation, **www.NewAmerica.net/ political reform**, (916) 448-3721

Midwest Democracy Center, **www.midwestdemocracy.org**, (312) 587-7060

The Reform Institute, **www.reforminstitute.org**, (703) 535-6897

Californians for Electoral Reform, **www.cfer.org**, (916) 455-8021

FairVote Minnesota, **www.fairvotemn.org**, (763) 807-2550

DemoChoice, **sf.demochoice.org** (online IRV poll)

4

Scrap Winner-Take-All Elections

When I worked for the Center for Voting and Democracy, we conducted a project interviewing current and former Illinois state legislators who had been elected by a non–winner-take-all method known as proportional representation (PR). Lessons from Illinois's use of this method for 110 years until 1980 have a lot to teach us about how to fix our broken democracy.

Many of the former legislators we interviewed were elder statesmen and stateswomen, most of them retired; it was a joy to listen to their reminiscences about Illinois politics. One interviewee was Abner Mikva, who had a distinguished career as a congressman, federal judge, law professor, and White House counsel for President Clinton. He first was elected to the Illinois House of Representatives in 1956 when they were using proportional representation.[1] What Judge Mikva and others had to say about Illinois's use of this system we will recognize as speaking directly to our national dilemmas of partisan polarization, little competition, regional balkanization, declining voter interest, and a loss of political ideas.

"[PR] gave the opportunity for outsiders like me to win a seat," said Mikva, an independent Democrat who ran against the Democratic Party machine in Chicago. "I never could have gotten elected if the party could have simply beat me one-on-one. I didn't have a lot of money." He said that under proportional representation, legislators were not so beholden to monied interests and political machines.

Said Mikva:

> You ended up with more independent people in the legislature. They weren't that responsible to a particular political party. Paul Powell couldn't dominate all of the Downstate Democrats because Paul Simon could get elected thanks to [proportional representation]. Richard Daley couldn't command all of the Cook County Democrats because Tony Scariano, Bob Mann, and others got elected. . . . The representatives in both parties had a lot more freedom. Everybody understood that you didn't have to toe a particular party line, or you didn't have to kowtow to a particular leader. So it generated a lot more independence within the legislature.[2]

Giddy Dyer, a GOP legislator for many years from the GOP stronghold of DuPage County, told us that, like Judge Mikva, she had to fight her own party's machine to get elected, and PR was indispensable.

> My county chairman was from the other branch, the right-wing branch of the Republican Party, and I would never have been quote "asked" to run by that county chairman. So when I decided to run, I really had to form my own campaign committee and not depend on the party for any help. . . . And Gene Hoffman in the neighboring district was in the same situation. He was a schoolteacher, and very strong on education, and from the moderate wing of the party, and he had to build his own organization to run.

Building your own electoral organization to run grassroots campaigns on a shoestring budget was possible with proportional representation. Illinois's particular method of PR used three-seat districts instead of single-seat districts. With PR and three-seat districts, it takes approximately one-quarter of the vote to win one seat. So an independent candidate could run and win without the backing of the party machine or a lot of money because she or he only needed support from one-quarter of the voters in the three-seat district. As a result, nearly every Illinois three-seat district had two-party representation. Said Mikva:

> [PR] gave a voice to a critical minority so that Democrats in the [heavily GOP] suburbs had a spokesperson from their district who they could rally around and generate some party activities. Similarly, in Chicago you had Republican representatives and these Republican outposts in a city that was dominated by the Democratic Party.

Mikva and Dyer saw other advantages to PR that addressed the dilemma of regional partisan balkanization and lopsided districts that turn entire regions into red and blue one-party fiefdoms.

Mikva: And the interesting thing is that within each district, if there was something that was really of local concern—a particular school, a particular public institution of some kind—because you had a representative of each of the parties in there, you could get that point of view expressed in *both* party caucuses. So that if Woodlawn Hospital wanted something, as a public institution in the district, not only could I and Representative Kennally be speaking within the Democratic Party caucus, Noble Lee could be speaking within the Republican Party caucus. So, in a sense it really gave the local, legitimate parochial concerns better presence and better voice than they have now.

Dyer: And I get back to the reason it's so important to have some Republican representatives from the city of Chicago is that they, many of them, had children in the Chicago public schools, and rode the CTA [metro transit system] and cared about Chicago's problems. And now, it seems to be polarized, between the city, the suburban ring, and downstate.

Mikva: This idea of balkanizing the state that way, it's not healthy. [Proportional representation], I think, helped us synthesize some of these differences, made us realize even though we were different than the downstaters, different than the suburbanites, that we also had a lot in common that held us together as a single state.

Because of PR, both parties won seats in all parts of the state. As a result, Republicans didn't ignore cities, and Democrats didn't ignore Republican strongholds. Illinois was not carved up into balkanized red and blue fiefdoms. In fact, for many years the Speaker of the House was a Democrat elected from heavily GOP DuPage County. When you only need 25 percent of the vote in a three-seat district to win a seat, Democrats in conservative areas and Republicans in liberal areas can still win representation.

Moreover, PR allowed for a broader spectrum of representatives *within* each party. A liberal region would elect two Democrats and one Republican, but the two Democrats often would be *two different types* of Democrats—a liberal Democrat and a moderate Democrat, or an independent Democrat and a conservative Democrat. Same with the Republicans. Voters all over the state, whether Democrats, Republicans, or independents, had a vote that counted for something. In Judge Mikva's Chicago district, one Democrat represented the Daley machine, Mikva represented a more independent Democratic perspective, and the dean of the John Marshall Law School was an elected Republican. According to Mikva:

> Between us we represented just about every organized point of view within the district. And that's something that you can't do with just one representative. If you represent the Democrats, the Republicans will feel voiceless; or you represent the organization, then the independents will feel voiceless. Or represent the conservatives, and the moderates

will feel voiceless. Whereas, with this multimember district, and particularly with [PR], it made it possible to give a legitimacy to the delegation that you don't have with single-member districts.

Harold Katz, former Democratic representative from the Chicago north suburb of Glencoe, a heavily GOP area, gets a gleam in his eye when he talks about PR. "The House [under proportional representation] was a very exciting place. It seemed to be the center of activity in the state capital. It was like a symphony, really, with not just two instruments playing, but a number of different instruments going at all times." John Porter, a Republican from the same area who later was elected to Congress, was so impressed by his experience of PR in Illinois's state government that he began working with other members of Congress to bring proportional representation to the federal government.

I thought it led to a much more independent and cooperative body that was not divided along party lines and run by a few leaders on each side. And it allowed individual legislators to work with members on both sides of the aisle in, I think, a very collegial atmosphere. . . . By its nature the system encouraged moderate viewpoints to be brought to bear. There's a great deal more independence for each member than there is under the present system.

Lee Daniels, former Republican Speaker of the Illinois House, has served in the state legislature for 30 years and has been elected under both PR with three-seat districts as well as a single-seat, winner-take-all system. He speaks with conviction about the advantages of proportional representation:

I thought it worked well. I thought it gave a guarantee of minority representation. In the Republican caucus, frequently we had Republican legislators talking about the needs of the city of Chicago. Today, generally speaking, there are very few Republicans that come from the city of Chicago so that the views of the city are very difficult to be communicated within our caucus. . . . I'm a great believer in representative democracy.

When listening to these Illinois legislators, Republican and Democrat alike, one quality that stands out is their belief that the other side deserves representation. They took seriously the Golden Rule of Politics: "Give unto others the representation you would have them give unto you." They believed it was good for their state's welfare and good for the political process. Compare that view to national politics today, the down and dirty game it has become where the Tom DeLays, Karl Roves, James Carvilles, and Dick Morrises will do whatever it takes to beat the other side.

But PR didn't serve only political minorities like Republicans in liberal areas and Democrats in conservative areas; it also helped women and racial minorities win representation. Barbara Flynn Currie has represented her Illinois district since the 1970s and is now House majority leader. She talks about how, as a result of proportional representation, her district became the first in Illinois history to send two women from the same party to the state legislature, herself and Carol Moseley Braun (Moseley Braun went on to be elected U.S. senator from Illinois). Adeline Geo-Karis, a Republican legislator who was elected both by PR and winner-take-all, agrees with Currie, saying PR "made it easier for women and minorities to get elected." Expanding on this viewpoint, Currie says, "In the days of [proportional representation], we had African Americans representing majority white districts, and white representatives coming from districts that were predominantly African American." PR helped elect black Republicans, but now the Republican Party in Illinois—like the rest of the nation—is virtually lily-white.

Might running in a larger three-seat district make campaigns more expensive? No, the legislators stated emphatically. Because you only need to win 25 percent of the vote, said Mikva, "you can appeal to a much smaller set of voters; that involves a much smaller amount of money being spent on them . . . advertising, media, so on." Campaign finance reformers should take note of the fact that candidates were able to run grassroots campaigns without the backing of their party machines or huge amounts of private money. With a lower victory threshold like 25 percent, money plays a much-reduced role. The experience of Emil Jones, Democratic Senate majority leader, illustrates the point. "The district I was elected from was a district that comprised only about 20 percent of African American constituencies. So, what I did was I organized the African American community. And, the other three candidates, they split the white vote, and I received a certain percentage of the white vote, and I ran second and won."

The GOP's Giddy Dyer perceptively summed up the problems with winner-take-all, including partisan gamesmanship and a lack of civility. "I think the lack of civility began when we did away with [proportional representation] and the multimember districts. Because now, it's just like two armies in full regalia fighting each other. There's just total squashing of many good ideas." The *Chicago Tribune*'s political reporter Rick Pearson has written that the rolling coalitions that formed in the Illinois House "often helped lead to centrist pragmatic policies."[3] Former Republican congressman Porter noted that in Illinois's three-seat districts with PR, "we operated in a less partisan environment because both parties represented the entire state." The *Chicago Tribune* has opined that "many partisans and political independents have looked back wistfully at [this] era. They acknowledge that it produced some of the best and brightest in Illinois politics."[4] Chicago's other daily, the *Sun-Times*, also has editorialized in favor of returning to proportional voting with three-seat districts.[5]

The Illinois story illustrates a provocative point that strikes at the very heart of our notions of "representation." Millions of orphaned voters—Republicans living in Democratic areas, Democrats in Republican areas, and third party supporters and independents everywhere—usually do not have a voice. But in Illinois under proportional representation, Republican legislators were elected in the blue liberal cities and Democrats in the red conservative areas. Independents, moderates, and the wings of the parties had a place at the table; so did women and minorities. In Illinois, Purple America had a home.

Unfortunately, this remarkable story had a downbeat turn. In 1980, a populist politician sponsored what was known as the Cutback Amendment—a statewide ballot measure that sought to "cut back" the size and cost of state government by shrinking the number of elected politicians by a third. This was at the dawn of the Reagan era, and the state legislature had just voted itself a sizable pay increase. With a populist battle cry of "get rid of the politicians," the Cutback Amendment won handily. Little recognized was that the ballot measure also did away with proportional voting. But the return to winner-take-all, single-seat districts caused the by-now-familiar litany of problems: little competition, regional balkanization, partisan polarization, low voter turnout, and so on. It virtually wiped out the Democratic Party in DuPage County and other conservative areas and killed the GOP in Chicago and other cities. It led to so many lopsided, one-party districts that in 2000, half of Illinois's House races were uncontested by one of the major parties. Another third of the House faced only token opposition. The return of winner-take-all elections also has led to an alarming concentration of power in what is known as the Four Tops—the majority and minority leaders in both the House and the Senate. According to the *Tribune*'s Pearson, the Four Tops now "use the cudgel of the potential loss of campaign cash to dictate the issues to be considered and how a member should vote. The formation of a true bipartisan coalition now is rare."[6]

In a hopeful sign, Judge Mikva and former Illinois GOP governor Jim Edgar cochaired a bipartisan commission in 2001 that strongly recommended a return to proportional representation.[7] A campaign in Illinois has begun called the "Drive to Revive," spearheaded by the Midwest Democracy Center with support from many state leaders and former legislators. So the Illinois story is far from over.

Another good sign is that many other places across the country are now using proportional methods, including Peoria, Illinois; Amarillo, Texas; Cambridge, Massachusetts; Hartford, Connecticut; and dozens of other local jurisdictions in South Dakota, Texas, and New Mexico.[8] Pennsylvania uses PR and three-seat districts to elect commissioners for most of its counties, and the commissions almost always have bipartisan representation. Proportional methods also are used to elect boards of directors for major corporations, including Hewlett-Packard, Sun Microsystems, PricewaterhouseCoopers, and Lockheed Martin. (For more explanation of the electoral rules of proportional representation, see this endnote.)[9]

The Illinois experience with proportional representation has a lot to teach us as we examine other political landscapes in the United States.

CALIFORNIA'S DILEMMA:
Achieving Representation for All

California is our nation's most populous state with over 35 million residents, more than the combined populations of our 21 least populous states. Its galloping level of diversity prefigures national trends: According to demographers, within a few decades the rest of the United States will look more like California today, and California will look more like . . . Mexico.

In the face of these sweeping demographic changes, California also faces a political crisis. Its political institutions and practices are failing. There are virtually no competitive races; in 2004, all incumbents were reelected to the state legislature, and all but two U.S. House races were won by landslides, with an average margin of victory of 42 percent. Voter turnout is among the lowest in the nation. Policy debate in Sacramento has degenerated into an antiquated battle between left and right, labor and business, taxes and subsidies. Moderate legislators have declined and have great difficulty performing their historic bridge-building role to shape bipartisan consensus. With 60 percent of California voters identifying themselves at the center of the political spectrum, nearly half of adults polled recently said Republicans and Democrats "do such a poor job that a third major party is needed."[10] This sentiment formed part of the amazing surge during the political rise of Arnold Schwarzenegger, who wore the mantle of a reformer. The time is ripe for significant and fundamental political reform. But what type of reform?

Consider the map of California on the next page, which shows which areas voted for John Kerry and which voted for President Bush in the 2004 presidential election. It looks the same as the map for Gore and Bush four years earlier, and it will look much the same for the Republican and Democratic candidates in 2008. As in so many states, the lack of competition can be traced to a combination of partisan residential patterns and the winner-take-all system. Regional partisan leanings in California have become entrenched over the past 20 years, with the heavily populated coastal areas and cities dominated by Democrats and the sparser interior dominated by Republicans. The result? Over 90 percent of California's legislative districts strongly favor one major political party over the other. But it's not due primarily to partisan redistricting and gerrymandered districts, as many have claimed. It's because California's residential patterns have balkanized into red and blue one-party fiefdoms. As we saw in Illinois, it is these partisan residential patterns combined with the single-seat district, winner-take-all system that is artificially dividing California into red and blue.

Counties won by John F. Kerry
Counties won by George W. Bush

2004 PRESIDENTIAL ELECTION RESULTS IN CALIFORNIA, BY COUNTY

Governor Schwarzenegger recognized some of these frustrating political dynamics and decided to do something about it. Unfortunately, he latched onto the wrong solution. He and his advisers decided to call a special election and sponsor a ballot initiative that would take redistricting out of the hands of the Democratic-controlled legislature and give it to an independent commission. But go back to the California map. Look again at the areas where Kerry won and where Bush won. The only way in California to make districts more competitive would be to use the Democratic urban areas as the hubs of a wheel and draw the districts as spokes radiating outward into the Republican interior. In southern California, there would need to be narrow districts beginning in downtown Los Angeles and extending east to Riverside and San Bernardino counties. In the Bay Area, the districts would need to begin in San Francisco and extend across the bay into Contra Costa County. Some of them would need to be narrow east-west bands up and down the state, extending from the Pacific Ocean to the Nevada-Arizona borders. But that kind of redistricting plan not only would look ridiculous but also would undermine the ability of "communities of interest" such as racial minorities to elect their representative, leading to legal challenges. It turns out there is a trade-off between creating more competitive districts and giving geographic minorities— whether political or racial, moderates or independents—a fair chance of electing representatives.

When this debate was raging in Governor Schwarzenegger's circles, I pointed out to members of the governor's cabinet the difficulties of creating competitive districts given these partisan residential patterns. I also pointed out that several states already were using the type of independent commissions Schwarzenegger and Common Cause were pushing for California, and the results were not encouraging. In Arizona, where an independent panel delineates districts, all eight congressional incumbents easily won reelection in 2004 with an average margin of victory of 34 percent. In the state senate, none of the 30 seats were competitive; in fact, more than half of the seats were uncontested by one of the two major parties (even though Arizona has public financing of elections, which should encourage more candidates). In Arizona, as it turns out, liberals and Democrats are more numerous in the southern part of the state around Tucson, while conservatives and Republicans dominate the rest of the state, including Phoenix. The only way to make winner-take-all districts more competitive would be to draw narrow bands that extended vertically from south to north, like the teeth of a fork.

Likewise, in Iowa, long considered the "poster child" of an effective redistricting commission, all congressional incumbents easily won reelection in 2004 with an average victory margin of 18 percent. In the state legislature, only 4 seats out of 100 were decided by less than a five-point victory margin, and the average margin was a whopping 47 percent. Other states using independent or bipartisan redistricting commissions (e.g., Washington, New Jersey) have had similarly disappointing results. Not that there aren't still some states where partisan gerrymanders have unfairly tilted the playing field, such as the GOP gerrymanders in Texas, Florida, Ohio, Pennsylvania, and Michigan.[11] But for most states, even ones such as Arizona and Iowa with independent redistricting commissions and public financing of elections (in Arizona), red and blue regional partisan demographics have bedeviled attempts to create more competitive races. In most states, demography has become destiny.

I told Schwarzenegger's circle that the roots of the dilemma go to the very heart of our political system, namely, representation based on geography—where you live—instead of what you think. California's use of a single-seat district, winner-take-all electoral system had reached its end game. Politics is about as good as it is going to get as long as California continues to use this antiquated winner-take-all method that is so ill suited for the New California and its wide range of attitudes, demographics, and geographic regions. Geographic representation, district elections, and winner-take-all methods may have been well suited for an 18th-century agrarian society that was dotted with small communities and connected by slow modes of communication and transportation. Geographic representation certainly was better than the alternative—the divine right of an autocratic and faraway king. But increasingly in the 21st century—in the mobile, multipartisan, multiracial, multireligious, multi–World Wide Webbed world we have become—the winner-take-all system is creating vexing problems.

To their credit, Governor Schwarzenegger and his advisers listened to my critique. Nevertheless, they pushed forward with their ill-fated ballot initiative to establish an independent commission that not only lost badly at the polls but even if passed would have accomplished very little. New approaches clearly are needed.

THE "NEW CALIFORNIA" PLAN

An Illinois-style proportional representation system holds great promise for California. PR would allow Republican/conservative voters to win representation in liberal urban areas and along the California coast, and liberal/Democratic voters to win representation in the rural and more conservative areas. It would interject a level of competition unknown in California politics, even electing more moderates, independents, and racial minorities without having to gerrymander districts. And it would result sometimes in representation for one of California's five ballot-qualified third parties. With more Californians represented by the candidates and parties they really like (instead of the lesser of two evils), and more voters mobilized by the increased level of political opportunity and campaign debate, voter turnout would increase.

Too good to be true? Consider the following scenario. Instead of electing 40 state senators from 40 districts that are one-party strongholds, as California does now, voters in 8 districts could elect 5 senators each. And instead of electing 80 assembly members from 80 safe-seat districts, voters in 16 districts could elect 5 representatives each (note that the number of legislators does not change). With an Illinois-type PR method, any candidate who won at least a sixth (about 17 percent) of the vote would earn one seat. A similar proportional method plan for California's congressional delegation has been designed by Fair-Vote (see the map on the next page, and www.fairvote.org/pr/super/2004/california.htm, for details). This plan likely would elect 28 Democrats and 17 Republicans with eight "swing seats" that could be won by either party. Latinos are well positioned to win nine seats, a 33 percent increase, more commensurate with their share of the population. Compare that to the status quo elected by California's current winner-take-all districts—0 swing seats, 6 Latinos, 34 Democrats, and 19 Republicans, nearly all won by huge landslide margins.

This proportional plan creates real competition. But it also allows geographic minorities, whether political or racial, to win representation in all parts of the state. For example, in District C, a five-seat district located in western, coastal Los Angeles that currently elects five Democrats to all five of those seats, a Republican candidate would win one at least one of the five seats. In District F, a five-seat district located in the interior "red" regions of southern California around Palm Springs and extending northward, which currently elects four Republicans and one Democrat, this district likely would elect two Republicans and two Democrats with one swing seat–leaning Republican, a fairer result mirroring the actual number of Republican and Democratic voters.

In district after district, Republican and Democratic voters would win fairer representation. Not only that, Democrats and Republicans would have incentive to vote and mobilize all the voters throughout the district to win that swing seat, an incentive that does not currently exist. All parts of the state would

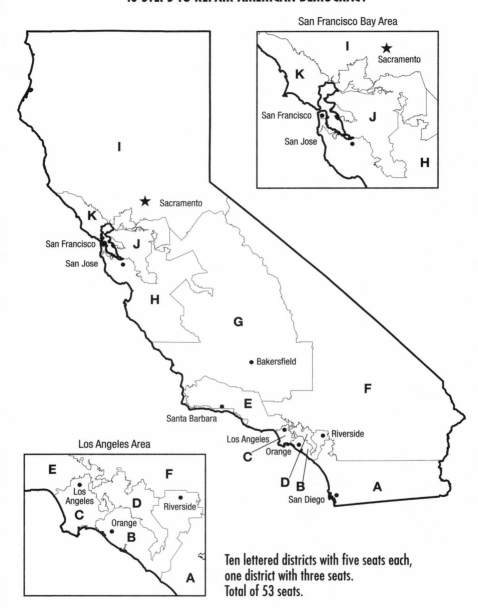

San Francisco Bay Area

Los Angeles Area

Ten lettered districts with five seats each,
one district with three seats.
Total of 53 seats.

THE NEW CALIFORNIA: A PROPORTIONAL
REPRESENTATION PLAN FOR 53 U.S. HOUSE SEATS

be competitive for both major political parties, and regional partisan balkanization would be significantly reduced. Occasionally an independent or third party candidate would reach the 17 percent threshold necessary to win one seat, further increasing competition and fostering even more political debate. Democratic and Republican moderates, including urban Republicans and rural Democrats, would be electorally viable. This in turn would encourage a cross-fertilization of ideas in the legislature and the political party caucuses, with the moderates acting as the bridge builders between the extremes. This is the only redistricting plan that fosters more competition and gives fairer representation to Democrats, Republicans, racial minorities, moderates, independent, and third party candidates, no matter where they live.

An Illinois-type PR system would go a long way toward producing a state legislature that not only better reflects the demographics of the New California but also is better prepared for the challenges of the 21st century. And it would accomplish all this without the backroom shenanigans of redistricting every 10 years. As proof of its broad appeal, two of the state's most influential daily newspapers, the *Sacramento Bee* and *San Jose Mercury News*, have written editorials favoring this sort of representation plan for California.[12]

FULL REPRESENTATION ACROSS THE NATION

At the national level, too, proportional representation has a lot to offer. Consider the situation in the South, where over the last two decades many blacks returned whose families previously had left the South. This homecoming of the black diaspora has resulted in nearly 55 percent of American blacks today living in the South, reinforcing the region's racial profile as mostly white-black.[13] But, the politics of the South have changed as well. The

"Solid South" used to be a Democratic Party stronghold; now it's largely red Republican country. White moderates have virtually disappeared from southern legislatures.[14] Of the 37 U.S. House members from the Deep South, 23 are conservative white Republicans, 9 are African American Democrats, and only 6 are white Democrats. Only three of 37 races were remotely competitive in 2004, as voters bunkered down in solidly red and blue winner-take-all districts, exacerbating the partisan and racial polarization.

Using proportional representation would lessen the degree of polarization. A typical three-seat district in the South (with a 25 percent victory threshold) likely would elect a white conservative Republican, a black liberal Democrat, and a relatively centrist Republican or Democrat. Besides electing more black Democrats and white moderates than the current method, such a plan almost certainly would elect more women—of 37 Deep South seats, women hold only 1. A black Republican or two might even get elected. Such full representation plans likely would increase the number of African Americans elected to the U.S. House in Virginia, North and South Carolina, Alabama, Louisiana, and possibly Arkansas without gerrymandering a single district. It would produce legislatures that more accurately reflect a typical southern electorate and the demographics of the New South.

If three-seat districts were used in other regions of the country, similar results would be seen. In New England, moderate Rockefeller Republicans, once a granitic mainstay of Yankee politics, could be viable again. In the Mountain and Prairie states, which used to elect populist Democrats such as Senators Frank Church from Idaho and Mike Mansfield from Montana but in recent years have experienced a virtual avalanche of Republican-dominated elections (though with recent Democratic gains in Montana and Colorado), Democrats would have more electoral opportunities. The resulting cross-fertilization in Republican and Democratic caucuses certainly would lessen some of the polarization and harsh rancor that now infects the Congress.

Representation in "Multi-Everything" Cities

Proportional voting methods also offer a fairer and more flexible method for achieving representation in diverse cities. In many ways, large metropolitan areas have become political worlds unto themselves. Today the urban zone, including the rapidly diversifying suburbs, is multiracial, multiethnic, multireligious, multicultural, multigendered, multipartisan—in short, "multi-everything." In the 21st century, what kinds of political structures will create a sense of shared community in these urban zones and lessen the level of tension? Although there are no easy answers to these questions, what is certain is that winner-take-all districts only exacerbate the problem. Nothing magnifies the turf wars more than a winner-take-all "if I win, you lose" form of politics. Redistricting battles in many cities have produced interracial bitterness as each minority group claws for its share of a limited commodity—political representation. The shortcomings of this approach are increasingly obvious.

Proportional voting methods offer a way out of this straitjacket. This potential was illustrated recently in an unlikely place: George W. Bush's backyard, the West Texas city of Amarillo. Although more than 20 percent of the city's population was black or Latino, no black or Latino candidates had been elected to the school board in more than two decades under the city's at-large winner-take-all elections. Instituted to settle a voting rights lawsuit, proportional voting had an immediate impact: Of the four open seats, one went to a black candidate and another to a Latino candidate, and voter turnout increased more than three times over that of the previous school board election. In the next election, another Latino was elected. Women won their first seats as well. Within two election cycles, Amarillo's school board became more representative without having to gerrymander a single district.[15]

Amarillo is not an isolated example. More than 100 jurisdictions across the country have adopted proportional methods, including more than 50 in Texas alone, often to resolve voting rights disputes.[16] In fact, in 1995 then-governor George W. Bush signed legislation allowing school districts to adopt proportional methods, attesting to the potential for cross-partisan appeal of these methods. Clearly as our cities—indeed, our entire nation—continue to "rainbowize," PR promises authentic representation to more individuals and constituencies as well as the best chance for a colorful mosaic that respects differences *and* knits them together into a more unified whole.

Nothing in the U.S. Constitution requires single-seat districts for the U.S. House, the 50 state legislatures, or local government. Ironically, there is one federal law—passed in 1967 to help elect more racial minorities—that mandates single-seat districts for U.S. House elections. By amending this federal law, states could be allowed to try proportional systems for their congressional representatives. State legislatures and city councils can do so now since they are not affected by that federal law. The more modern proportional voting methods offer the best hope for facilitating fair representation in the 21st century, directly addressing our national, state, and local dilemmas of partisan polarization, regional balkanization, little competition, loss of political ideas, declining voter interest, and an out-of-touch government.

CRITICISMS OF PROPORTIONAL REPRESENTATION

Economist Kenneth Arrow won a Nobel Prize for proving there's no such thing as a perfect electoral system. All such systems have their ups and downs, but some have more ups and fewer downs. There are different types of proportional systems with names such as party list voting, choice voting, cumulative voting, and more. Certain proportional systems are based on voting for individual candidates; others are party based. Some proportional democracies in Europe and elsewhere use large multiseat districts—the size of their entire country—while others use smaller, moderately proportional three- to seven-seat districts. Some European democracies have constructed the electoral rules to allow a multiplicity of political parties (some say too many parties); others use electoral rules that limit their multiparty democracy to four or five political parties winning seats in the legislature.

The number of elected political parties is purely a function of the "victory threshold" used, which is chosen by those designing the electoral system. If you use a low victory threshold, where it takes only, say, 1 percent of the vote to win a legislative seat, you will see a proliferation of political parties—perhaps too many. However, if you use a higher threshold such as the 5 to 17 percent threshold used by various nations, you will see what is called "moderate proportional representation," with approximately four to six political parties with any chance of getting elected (two of these being major parties, one center-left and one center-right, and two to four smaller parties that wax and wane in influence depending on the issues of the day; see the endnote for more explanation).[17]

Many reporters, pundits, and political scientists point to Italy or Israel to illustrate the downsides of PR. They note those democracies have been held hostage by minority parties that precipitated the collapse of coalition governments. But Israel for many years required only 1 percent of the vote to win a seat, which certainly was too low for Israel (though it's worked fine in South Africa) and allowed religious parties too much political leverage. And collapsing coalition governments like in Italy and Israel are not something we have to worry about in the United States since those are caused by the use of a parliamentary system, not proportional representation, and we don't use a parliamentary system in the U.S. So these criticisms of Israel and Italy are not very applicable to the American situation, especially when using three- to five-seat districts with moderately proportional victory thresholds of 17 to 25 percent instead of 1 percent.

Ironically, the critics also don't recognize that, under our own winner-take-all system, small slices of the most zealous parts of the electorate ("the base") and the least informed and most detached part of the electorate ("the swing voters") also acquire exaggerated power. In fact, those small wedges of voters can determine which party wins the presidency if they tilt the results in even one battleground state such as Florida or Ohio. So our own system is very much undermined by extremist politics. Reducing the vast research literature on proportional representation to the perceived troubles of Italy or Israel is no more legitimate than reducing the drawbacks of winner-take-all to the troubles of winner-take-all democracies like Algeria, Angola, or India. In fact, proportional systems are used by *most* of the established democracies in the world today. Of the 45 nations with at least two million inhabitants and high human rights ratings from Freedom House, only a handful, including the United States, do not use some kind of proportional voting system to elect at least one of their national legislatures.[18] Among the many democracies that use PR, few experience the difficulties of Italy and Israel.

In fact, the trend around the world is decidedly away from our winner-take-all system and toward proportional systems. The fledgling democracies of South Africa and in the former Soviet bloc rejected many of our key political practices and methods, particularly our winner-take-all voting system, the archaic Electoral College, and an unrepresentative upper chamber (e.g., the U.S. Senate) invested with so much power. New Zealanders recently discarded winner-take-all after using it for 150 years and chose the German form of proportional representation. Even our own political progenitor, the United Kingdom, is midstream of an astonishing political transformation, having recently adopted PR for electing representatives to the European Parliament, the London City Council, the Scottish and Wales regional assemblies, and Scottish local councils. Some political observers predict it is only a matter of time before the House of Commons scraps its winner-take-all elections, too.

No rule or law says we cannot combine our single-seat districts with proportional representation, offering the benefits of both, as Germany, New Zealand, and Japan have done. Roughly speaking, a district's geographic orientation gives representation based on where you *live*, while proportional representation gives representation based on what you *think*. These approaches are not mutually exclusive; indeed, they can be complementary. Our bicameral state legislatures provide an easy opening for such a mixed system. We could use geographic-based representation via winner-take-all districts in one house of the legislature, and proportional representation where voters win representation based on what they think in the other.

STEPS TOWARD REFORM

The question is, How do we move forward? In addition to all the usual processes for creating a change of this magnitude— lobbying legislators, endorsements from leaders and organizations, working locally and building momentum, voter initiatives, mobilizing constituencies, and so on—one of the most promising vehicles for reform was on display not that long ago across the border in Canada. It's called a Citizens Assembly, and it was pioneered in 2004–2005 in British Columbia. The government there turned over to average citizens the task of basic political reform and by doing so took the partisanship and incumbent protectionism out of the process, something the United States badly needs. Here's how it worked.

The government randomly selected 160 people to participate in the Citizens Assembly, like selecting a jury pool. The Assembly had 80 women and 80 men, one of each from all the provinces 79 electoral districts, plus two seats added for native

85

Canadians. It was an independent, nonpartisan body charged with a particular focus: to examine British Columbia's electoral system and how their winner-take-all system was performing. This effort was unique. Often such task forces are dominated by the usual political insiders or good government activists. Nowhere in the world had randomly selected citizens with no history of interest in electoral reform been so empowered to shape major proposals. Yet the work of the Assembly was unanimously endorsed by the political parties in the legislature and community leaders, who granted it generous funding.

The Assembly's tenure was divided into three phases over 11 months, meeting on weekends, for which they were paid about $1000 per month. They were addressed by top experts from all political perspectives who gave them the benefit of their knowledge and analysis. They held over 50 public hearings around the province. The Assembly delivered a final report in December 2004, voting 146 to 7 to toss out its longtime winner-take-all, single-seat district electoral system and replace it with a multi-seat proportional representation system. "This really is power to the people," enthused Jack Blaney, the chair of the Citizens Assembly.

The Assembly's proposal was submitted by the legislature directly to the voters in a referendum in May 2005. Because the Citizens Assembly was composed of average citizens, its recommendation had tremendous legitimacy with the public. A robust 58 percent of voters supported the measure—but it needed 60 percent to pass. However, the strong yes vote unleashed a wave of sentiment, resulting in the government putting the question back on the ballot for 2008 and funding a province-wide educational effort.

The Citizens Assembly in British Columbia focused on the electoral system, but the focus could have been on other aspects of the political system, such as redistricting, campaign finance, term limits, or the broken primary system. The Citizens Assembly solves a real dilemma: how do we enact meaningful political reform, which the United States so badly needs, when both political parties have conflicts of interest that induce them to manipulate the rules in their favor? Citizens Assemblies could be important vehicles for modernizing our political system because trust is placed in average citizens who have more credibility than the political class. The popularity of Citizens Assemblies has spread, with three other Canadian provinces, Ontario, Quebec, and New Brunswick, launching their own versions.[19] Citizens Assemblies are being considered in Australia, the Netherlands, and the UK. In January 2006, a bill was introduced into the state legislature to create a California Citizens Assembly. Now is the time to inject fairness and nonpartisanship into our politics, and what better way than by establishing Citizens Assemblies at local, state, and federal levels that empower average citizens to decide what political reform is best?

As a partial, strategic step toward proportional representation, some jurisdictions may want to begin with instant runoff voting first, or perhaps fusion, which is used in New York and a few other states and allows political parties to cross-endorse each other's candidates on separate ballot lines. In New York, the smaller Conservative Party can endorse the Republican Party's candidate, and that candidate will appear on the ballot line for both parties; the Working Families Party or Green Party can do the same with Democrats. Where it has a strong candidate, the third party runs independent campaigns; otherwise, it fuses with the major party candidate. Like instant runoff voting, fusion gives smaller parties a foothold in a two-party system. It gets voters used to voting for the third party and legitimizes a multiparty field.

However we get the job done, the important point is to begin the transition from our antiquated winner-take-all system to the more modern proportional representation. It is ironic that American businesses are extolled for innovation and modernization, yet when it comes to our politics, we are hopelessly bogged down by tradition and the status quo. It is crucial that we modernize our representative democracy, and in that process the considerable deficiencies of our 18th-century winner-take-all system must be front and center. Proportional voting systems— not winner-take-all—must provide the political engine for American democracy in the 21st century.

▇ Summary of Recommendations

1. Scrap winner-take-all elections: use proportional representation for electing local, state, and federal legislatures.
2. Recognize that redistricting reforms and independent redistricting commissions won't accomplish much in most states—partisan residential patterns are trumping line drawers' ability to affect elections.
3. Create Citizens Assemblies as a reform vehicle that removes partisanship and incumbent protectionism.
4. Use instant runoff voting and fusion as partial steps toward proportional representation.

▇ Organizations to Contact

FairVote, **www.fairvote.org**, (301) 270-4616

New America Foundation, **www.newamerica.net/ politicalreform**, (202) 986-2700

Working Families Party (for fusion), **www.workingfamiliesparty.org/fusion.html**

Californians for Electoral Reform, **www.cfer.org**, (916) 455-8021

FairVote Minnesota, **www.fairvotemn.org**, (763) 807-2550

······**5**······

Direct Election of the President

Wherever I went on the lecture or radio talk show circuit following the 2000 election, the subject of the Electoral College inspired widespread confusion. Many Americans, even if they accepted or were pleased by the results of that election, shook their heads over this odd way of electing the president. And Europeans were completely perplexed. I gave a lecture at London's Conway Hall, a historical venue where abolitionists, suffragists, George Bernard Shaw, and old Fabians once inveighed against the injustices of their day. One questioner inspired a lot of head nods: "How is it that a candidate with fewer votes could win? Or that a state like California, with something like 70 times more people than Wyoming, has only 18 times the number of electoral votes? It seems that the votes of people in Wyoming are worth a lot more than the votes of Californians—odd that, wouldn't you say?"

I was impressed that a Brit should be so knowledgeable about the American political system, more so than most Americans. "Yes, I know it seems peculiar," I replied. "But in America's method of electing the president—well, yes, some voters are worth more than others. A lot more."

I explained how our Electoral College system gives each state an electoral vote for each member of the U.S. House of Representatives (which is based on population) and for each U.S. senator (two senators per state, regardless of population). The practical effect of this arrangement is to give low-population states such as Wyoming more electoral votes per capita than high-population states such as California. A lot more. The 170 or so audience members groaned and shook their heads. "It's as bad as our House of Lords," commented one person, to more head nods. After all, they had just witnessed the most powerful leader in the world elected under dubious circumstances. To those not steeped in the mythologies of the Founders and Framers and their 18th-century creation, these sorts of oddities look more than confusing; they look unfair and bizarre. Why should an electoral method weigh Americans' votes differently based on where they live? Isn't America the "land of equality," after all?

Some of the examples illustrating the idiosyncrasies of our Electoral College system do look bizarre. For example, about 26 million people live in the 11 western and mountain states of Montana, Wyoming, Nevada, North and South Dakota, Colorado, Nebraska, Kansas, Oklahoma, Alaska, and Arizona—a vast yet sparse region of fiery GOP red stretching from the Canadian to the Mexican borders. That's about the same population as the northeastern states of New York and Massachusetts. But in the 2000 election, those 11 states had nine more electoral votes than New York and Massachusetts, all of which went to George W. Bush. That factor alone was enough to hand victory to Bush.

In 1789, when General George Washington took the oath of office as the first president of the United States, the ratio between the most populous state (Virginia) and the least populous (Delaware) was only 11 to 1.[1] Now it is 70 to 1, and increasing. The Framers simply did not foresee such dramatic population imbalances 200 years later. Consequently, the Electoral College method they have saddled us with gives the people of Wyoming *four times* the per capita representation of Californians in the Electoral College. The regions of the country growing the fastest are experiencing the greatest loss of representation. So much for "equality for all" or "one person, one vote."

The "one person, one vote" principle is derived from two Supreme Court rulings in the early 1960s, *Baker v. Carr* and *Reynolds v. Sims*, which interpreted the Fourteenth Amendment

90

to mean that the number of representatives per capita must be equal from legislative district to legislative district to ensure that everyone's vote will be worth the same amount of "democracy power." The Electoral College essentially is a legislature, with each state as the legislative "district" and multiple "representatives" called electors. Yet as a legislature, the Electoral College, as well as the United States Senate (see the next chapter), completely violate the "one person, one vote" principle because some states have far more electors per capita than others.

Following the 2000 election, the most immediately obvious defect of the Electoral College appeared to be that a candidate who loses the popular vote could win the electoral vote. Historically, though, the Electoral College has seated only four second-place winners, perhaps not a bad record over 200-plus years. But we need to look deeper. In 18 elections—one out of three presidential contests—the United States has ended up with a winner who won the most votes but lacked a popular majority.[3] A shift of less than 1 percent of the national vote in several additional elections would have handed the presidency to candidates losing the popular vote. In 2004, a shift of fewer than 60,000 votes in Ohio would have elected John Kerry despite his losing the national popular vote by 3 million votes. Particularly in the 49–49 nation, with the two sides so close, another meltdown in our Electoral College method could be just around the corner.

OTHER ELECTORAL COLLEGE DEFECTS IN THE 49–49 NATION

The Electoral College has three other significant defects in a closely divided nation, none of which has received as much attention as the problem of nonmajority winners.

Presidential elections have become a spectator sport. Though national elections are so close, the irony is that fewer and fewer

Americans play a meaningful role in deciding who's elected president. That's because our Electoral College structure enables campaigns to ignore safe states and to focus on a handful of battleground states. Most states today are safe, and the last two presidential elections boiled down to Ohio and Florida. So will the 2008 presidential election. Most of the other states and the voters who live in those states watched the 2000 and 2004 elections as spectators from the 42nd row.

That's because the Electoral College method of electing the president uses a winner-take-all allocation: All electoral votes in a state are awarded to whichever candidate wins the highest number of votes, whether by one vote or one million, even if that candidate didn't win a majority of the statewide vote (Maine and Nebraska also use a winner-take-all allocation, but it's broken down by congressional district).[4] That makes the presidential election in each state another "If I win, you lose" proposition, just like our legislative elections. Republican voters in solidly blue states and Democratic voters in solidly red states may as well not have showed up to the polls, for all their votes mattered.

And it is not just Democrats and Republicans in the wrong states whose votes don't count. It's also the supporters of independents and third party candidates everywhere. And also most black voters, since 55 percent of all blacks live in southern states where they were outvoted easily in 2000 and 2004 by the more numerous white voters for Bush. Bush won every southern state and every border state except Maryland, so the southern white vote completely erased the massive black turnout in the South. Additionally, white voters are far more likely than racial minorities to live in battleground states—more than 30 percent of the nation's white population live in the influential battleground states, but less than 20 percent of minorities do.[5] So there is a strong but overlooked racial dimension to the Electoral College landscape.

Significantly, the number of battleground states has decreased in recent years, which means the number of spectator states—and ignored voters—has increased. In 1960, 24 states with a total of 327 electoral votes were battlegrounds. In 2004, only 13 states with 159 electoral votes (and a mere 27 percent of the nation's population) were even remotely competitive.[6] In fact, six months before the election, the experts knew the final result was going to boil down to only two states: Ohio and Florida.[7] Two-thirds of the states didn't see a TV ad, get a visit from a candidate, or experience much of a campaign presence. But residents of Ohio, where the Bush and Kerry campaigns along with allied PACs spent an unprecedented $47 million in TV advertising in October and November, or Florida, inundated with $64 million during that period, were getting carpet-bombed night after night by a "shock and awe" TV blitzkrieg.[8] Not surprisingly, voter turnout in the most competitive states increased at four times the rate of the least competitive states, and voter turnout among 18- to 29-year-olds was on average 17 points higher in the 10 most competitive states.[9]

Not only are fewer states involved in deciding the winner, but fewer voters *within* those battleground states are the decisive voters. Campaigns confine their targeted messaging to two narrow slices of voters: either undecided swing voters or already-decided base voters. The first group you try to persuade and swing your way; the second you try to mobilize and swell the numbers. In recent years, the Republican Party has targeted its efforts to turning out the vote from an expanding base of partisans, while the Democrats still focus more on the swing voters.[10] The candidates use modern campaign techniques to precisely aim their TV ads like missiles at their targeted audience, bombarding the airwaves in a handful of swing states. Meanwhile, all is quiet on the safe-state front, which is most of the country. And what should be a national election boils down to a handful of voters in a handful of states determining the winner.

Elections are more likely to be decided by administrative error or fraud. In an era of close presidential elections, the continued

93

use of the Electoral College increases the chances of a presidential election decided by election administrative screwups or outright fraud. The last two presidential elections have illustrated this point in alarming fashion. For instance, for George W. Bush to have won the national popular vote in 2000, he would have needed to change the results of over a half million votes. But with the Electoral College system, with Florida decided by only 537 votes, the winner needed to change the results of fewer than 600 votes in one state—by whatever means necessary.

Recall the horrendous butterfly ballot—by all accounts an honest mistake by a Democratic election official in Palm Beach County, Florida, which ended up confusing thousands of Democratic voters into voting for Pat Buchanan instead of Al Gore and costing Gore the election. Recall Walden O'Dell, CEO of Diebold Election Systems, one of the nation's largest manufacturers of voting equipment, who moonlighted as a major Bush fund-raiser and stated that "we are going to deliver Ohio to the president" even as his company was seeking millions of dollars in Ohio contracts for voting equipment. And who can forget Katherine Harris, the infamous chief election officer in Florida who also was cochair of the "Elect George W. Bush" committee. In the 2000 election, she was involved in suspicious activities such as manipulating felony voting lists to disqualify thousands of Florida blacks—likely Democratic voters—from the ballot. Perhaps nothing crooked occurred in any of these episodes. But when a change of 600 votes out of 100 million can alter the outcome of an election, common sense tells you that it's a temptation that can lead to serious problems. With 51 separate state and District of Columbia contests for the presidency, the odds are increased that in a close election, narrow margins will arise in enough states that the conduct of elections will be controversial—and end up in court. Even in 2004, when Bush won the nationwide popular vote by more than three million votes, the serious voting irregularities in Ohio's close election led to expensive litigation and suspicions that the results were not fair. Given today's hardening partisan divisions, expect even more controversy and litigation in our elections. Too much is riding on a handful of votes in a handful of states.

The small-state subsidy favors conservative candidates. Due to the peculiar nature of the apportionment of votes in the Electoral College, our presidential elections defy the fundamental principle of "one person, one vote" by giving more electoral votes per capita to low-population states. Most of these are conservative red states, which in turn gives an advantage to Republican presidential candidates over Democrats. That's why Al Gore could win a half million more votes for president in 2000 yet lose the presidency. George W. Bush won more of the low-population states with 3, 4, or 5 electoral votes and benefited from their representation subsidy, winning the electoral vote by a razor-thin 271–267. Moreover, Bush's small states are so solidly red that a Republican does not need to make any effort to win there—Kerry won 40 percent or less in 13 states and less than 30 percent in Wyoming and Utah. So those outcomes freed Bush to concentrate on the battleground states, much more so than Kerry, giving him an additional advantage.

Law professor Vikram Amar and others dispute that the Electoral College structure lopsidedly favors Republican candidates. While he agrees that Republicans benefit from the small-state skew, he says that the Electoral College also helps the Democrats by exaggerating the power of big states via the winner-take-all rules. Certainly it is true that while Kerry and Bush each won 7 of the 14 largest states, Kerry's states had a solid electoral vote advantage of 37 votes, primarily due to the strong Democratic lock on California, New York, and Illinois. Certainly scenarios are possible where a Democrat could lose the national popular vote and win the Electoral College vote, including in 2004 when a swing of only 60,000 votes in Ohio would have elected John Kerry with 3 million fewer nationwide votes than President Bush.

Overall, however, the Republicans must be pleased with the political geography of the Electoral College map. Having a national election come down to states such as Ohio, Florida, New Mexico, Iowa, and Nevada, instead of a national direct election where Democrats could mobilize more voters in solidly blue states such as California, New York, and Illinois, does not play to the Democrats' strong suit. Think of Hillary Clinton trying to win the presidency by rallying blue-collar workers in Ohio and Florida to beat John McCain or Rudy Giuliani, and you can see the shakiness of the Democrats' position.

But even more important than a built-in Republican advantage is that the Electoral College does not work for the American people. It means that the losing candidate can be the winner and that the political landscape favors one party's candidates over the other. It means that some voters are worth more than others because votes are weighed differently, depending on where you live. In a nation that professes the democratic principles of "the majority rules" and "one person, one vote," our presidential election method utterly fails those tests.

IN DEFENSE OF THE ELECTORAL COLLEGE—NOT!

Defenders of the Electoral College typically boil their reasons down to two: (1) It means candidates cannot ignore less populous states because those states have more votes per capita, and (2) "it militates against regional parties" because you have to win 51 individual contests across the nation, which helps achieve a national consensus.[11] These two reasons have a considerable amount of currency with many political scientists and pundits, yet they are demonstrably false. As we have seen, the political parties and their candidates' election results are indeed breaking down regionally, with alarming balkanized voting patterns displayed in both the 2004 and 2000 presidential elections. Moreover, even a cursory study of presidential campaigns shows that candidates in fact *do* ignore most low-population states. That's because most of these low-population states are solidly locked up for one party.

In fact, Bush's reelection strategist Matthew Dowd remarked in 2004 that the campaign, despite having more resources than any other in history, had not polled outside the 18 closest states in more than two years. The ignored states included most low-population states, including entire regions in the South and West.[12] Even in the few battleground states, the candidates spent far more time in the populous states of Ohio and Florida than in sparse New Mexico, Iowa, or Nevada. When a national election boils down to a handful of states, regionalism has triumphed, and the election ceases to be a vehicle for national consensus.

Another defense of the Electoral College amounts to little more than "If the Founders created it, then it must be right." According to this fundamentalist view, the Framers' brilliance has shone down through the centuries, and the preeminence of the United States in the world is proof of the majesty of their constitutional creation. However, a reading of the actual proceedings of the Constitutional Convention refutes any notion that the Electoral College method was founded on brilliant political theory or inspired design. The eminent political scientist Robert Dahl has narrated the story of the Constitutional Convention in his enlightening book *How Democratic Is the American Constitution?* As he makes clear, the confused and baffled delegates debated proposal after proposal, none of them satisfying. Finally, they simply ran out of time and ideas, and in desperation, a much-divided body chose a slightly tweaked version of a proposal they previously had rejected.[13] But within the first few presidential elections, their last-minute improvisation had broken down, prompting an immediate constitutional amendment (the Twelfth Amendment). Thus, a defense of the Electoral College that relies on extolling the brilliance of the Framers is no defense at all. The Framers were mere mortals after all, and while their clunky creation was better than the divine right of an autocratic king, it had considerable defects that the American nation has been grappling with ever since.

THE SOLUTION:
National Direct Election of the President

For more than 50 years, a Gallup poll has shown that a large majority of Americans wants to scrap the Electoral College and adopt a direct national election of the president. In every election in this country, we adhere to the principle of "one person, one vote"—except when it comes to the presidency and the U.S. Senate, both 18th-century relics of the Founders' invention. But the U.S. Congress, which is charged with passing constitutional amendments on to the state legislatures by a two-thirds vote of each chamber, has been unresponsive to the common sense of the public.

The advantages of a direct election are clear. First, it gets rid of this troublesome parallel system where the loser of the popular vote can still win the Electoral College vote. With a direct national election, one vote by the people will get the job done. Second, it gets rid of safe states and spectator voters. Suddenly all voters count no matter where they live, as do all states. Sure, candidates will have a tendency to go to the big media markets where most of the people live, which is one of the fears of those opposed to a national direct election. But they already do this now, except they do it in a handful of battleground states rather than across the country. In a close national direct election, candidates will have incentive to visit many of the ignored states, even the less populous states, because they will need every vote to win. You will see Republican candidates campaigning in Illinois, New York, Connecticut, Delaware, and other blue states, and Democratic candidates appearing in Texas, Georgia, Montana, Idaho, and other red states—something that doesn't happen right now. In fact, with the current method, even the winning parties don't go to those states. So a national direct election better addresses one of the concerns of Electoral College defenders: It will make our presidential election more of a nationwide contest.

A national direct election will reenergize voters all across the country, no matter their political persuasion. Tens of millions of spectator voters currently residing in one-party states would have reason to vote. Candidates would have incentive to turn out a nationwide vote, producing turnout surges in more areas of the country like those we see only in battleground states today. This would make more voters excited again, eager to participate, as they realized their vote was important toward their candidate's national total no matter where they live.

Also, a national direct election would make it nearly impossible for a close national election to be decided by an administrative mistake or—heaven forbid—fraud. You would have to change too many votes in too many places in order to make a difference. For instance, it would be statistically impossible for the race to be decided by a poorly designed ballot of one county elections clerk, as happened in the 2000 election with the butterfly ballot in Palm Beach County, Florida. And with 100 million votes being cast, fraud committed in a dozen counties in one, two, or three states out of the more than 3,000 counties nationwide is not going to change election results. So a national direct election is an insurance policy against election fraud or administrative screwups. Whatever their motives, the Katherine Harrises and Walden O'Dells would have diminished impact.

Finally, unlike the Electoral College method that favors Republican candidates, a national direct election of more than 100 million voters would have no built-in bias in favor of one political party or one geographic region over another. All votes would be weighed the same no matter where you live. All candidates from all political parties would be on equal footing—go out there, all across the country, and win as many votes as you can. That's the fair way to conduct an election and also the most transparent. A direct national election would not leave Americans and foreign observers shaking their heads over a confusing and suspicious-looking procedure.

Some worry that a national election would lead to multiple Florida-type debacles with recounts required all over the country. But this scenario is extremely unlikely. Statistically speaking, even with the two sides so close in the 49–49 nation, with more than 100 million votes up for grabs, a national election almost never would be so close that the results wouldn't be definitive. France directly elects its president with more than 25 million voters participating, and never has there been an election so close that it required recounts all over the country. If a recount ever were necessary, Washington's gubernatorial race in 2004 showed it's doable: Election officials had to hand-recount all 2.8 million ballots in a race decided by a mere 129 votes. But more efficient recount procedures are available that could be used and that don't involve recounting the entire country. All told, the benefits of a national direct election for president, election after election, far outweigh any potential downsides.

Majority Requirement

One indispensable feature that must accompany a national direct election is a requirement that the winner receive a majority of the national popular vote. If a candidate wins with less than a majority, we can't be certain that candidate was preferred by the most voters. As we saw in 2000 with Ralph Nader on the ballot and in 1992 with Ross Perot, whenever you have more than two candidates, the possibility exists of split votes, and spoiling that can result in the wrong candidate winning. So a majority requirement is essential.

There are two ways to ensure majority winners. One way is by using a runoff election between the top two finishers, as the French use for their presidential election. But this approach requires a second election, which has downsides. First, it is expensive for taxpayers, who must foot the bill for the costs of holding the second election; it also is expensive for candidates, who must raise more money to run a second election, undermining campaign finance reform. Second, it usually leads to increased mudslinging and hack-attack campaigning in the head-to-head combat of the face-off election, a real turnoff for voters. Third, usually a change in voter turnout occurs between the first and second elections (resulting partly from the mudslinging campaigns) that has a tendency to further disenfranchise chronically undermobilized constituencies such as racial minorities, young people, and the poor.

So the best majoritarian method is instant runoff voting, as discussed in chapter 3. It's a fairer, faster, and cheaper alternative to the two-round runoff method. With IRV, voters rank their runoff choices at the same time as their first choice, 1, 2, 3, and the runoff rankings are used to elect a majority winner in a single election. Instant runoff voting really is the most democratic method, but either of these runoff methods is heads and shoulders above what we do now to elect our president.

HOW TO ADOPT A NATIONAL DIRECT ELECTION

Reforming the Electoral College will not be easy because the low-population states that benefit from its structure have a near-veto over any constitutional amendments. However, opinion polls show a strong majority of Americans are in favor of scrapping the Electoral College. So the low-population states have their finger in the dike, holding back the tide of public opinion.

Most of the resistance to reform presumably will come from Republicans, since they are in power. But if a mere 60,000 voters in Ohio had changed their minds and voted for Kerry, he would have won the presidency even while losing the national popular vote by 3 million votes. That would have made believers in direct national elections out of many Republicans. GOP leaders such as Senators Strom Thurmond, Orrin Hatch, and John McCain have supported reforming or abolishing the Electoral College, so one should not assume that Republican support is impossible. And Democrats already have ample reason to support such a move: After all, the Electoral College method denied Al Gore the presidency in 2000, even though he won the most votes nationwide. Senator Dianne Feinstein and Representative Jesse Jackson Jr. both have introduced constitutional amendments to abolish the Electoral College and institute direct election of the president. Representative Jackson's includes a requirement that the president should win with a majority of the nationwide popular vote, and that's the best approach.

Until momentum builds behind a constitutional amendment, halfway solutions can move the effort forward more quickly. One way would be to adopt, state by state, instant runoff voting for the allocation of each state's electors. This can be done by changing state law—no constitutional amendments are needed. Any state that adopts IRV at least will ensure that its awarding of electoral votes won't be plagued by spoiler candidates, split votes among like-minded voters, or nonmajority winners. For instance, in the 2000 election, nine states gave all their electoral votes to a candidate lacking a majority of the popular vote, including Florida and New Hampshire, where the wrong candidate won as a result. A change to IRV in either state would have given the presidential election to Gore. In the 1992 presidential election, a whopping 49 states were won by a candidate lacking a popular majority because of the presence of Ross Perot on the ballot. It's possible that a state-by-state use of IRV may have elected a different president that year.

The most promising effort in the short term is an innovative approach that has been proposed by a reform organization called National Popular Vote, with the support of organizations including Common Cause and FairVote. It has devised a clever way to enact a national direct election without a constitutional amendment. It utilizes the ability of states to enter into treaties with each other, as well as the fact that the U.S. Constitution reserves to the state legislature the power to decide how to allocate the electors. The state legislature for each signatory state would agree to give all its electors to whichever candidate won the national popular vote. Once a critical mass of states together wielding a majority of electoral votes (currently at least 270) had agreed to the treaty, it would go into effect among all those states, and the presidential election would become a de facto national popular vote. This method also has the advantage of being enacted on a state-by-state basis, yet it would not require a three-fourths vote in the state legislatures or a two-thirds vote in both houses of Congress as a constitutional amendment needs. It could be passed by a simple majority vote in each state legislature. This effort is analogous to how states took the lead in moving to direct election of U.S. senators or women's right to vote, with the people in each state forcing their state legislatures to respect the popular will.

Those who care about democracy and the fairness of our presidential elections should begin working in their state to change how we elect the president. The United States should demonstrate that basic democratic principles such as equality, majority rule, and "one person, one vote" are as important to Americans as we say they should be to new democracies. Scrapping the Electoral College will help make the United States a modern democracy ready for the 21st century instead of being stuck in the 18th. It's time for the Electoral College to go.

▇ Summary of Recommendations

1. Pass a constitutional amendment creating a national direct election for president using a majority requirement (elected by instant runoff voting).
2. Take intermediate steps toward a national direct election:
   - Each state passes a law to use instant runoff voting for its presidential election.
   - Each state passes a law to use a proportional allocation of electors, instead of winner-take-all.
   - States cosign a treaty awarding their electors to the winner of the national popular vote.

▇ Organizations to Contact

National Popular Vote, **www.nationalpopularvote.com**

FairVote, **www.fairvote.org**, (301) 270-4616

Common Cause, **www.commoncause.org**, (202) 833-1200

U.S. PIRG, **www.uspirg.org**, (202) 546-9707

6

Overhaul the U.S. Senate

James Madison, the "Father of the Constitution" and our fourth president, and Alexander Hamilton, the first secretary of the treasury and architect of the new republic's financial system, were two of the most important participants in the Constitutional Convention. After the Constitution was drafted, Madison and Hamilton (along with John Jay) wrote a series of influential essays in favor of ratification, now known famously as the *Federalist Papers*. So when patriotic defenders of the Constitution speak with reverence about the Founders and Framers, Madison and Hamilton are at the head of the pack.

Yet both Madison and Hamilton opposed the creation of one of our most fundamental institutions—the United States Senate. They spoke strongly against the apportionment scheme that gave two senators to each state, regardless of population. Their primary reason for opposing this apportionment, still relevant today, was its "unjustifiable limit on national majorities."[1] This meant that awarding two senators per state, regardless of population, could plausibly result in a minority of voters winning a majority of Senate seats. Not only did this practice undermine the principle of what later became known as "one person, one vote," but it meant that the Senate could become a real barrier to enacting policies supported by a majority of Americans. This scenario contradicted many of the basic reasons for founding the United States.

The speeches and writings produced by Hamilton, Madison, and others opposing the Senate were strongly worded. One

Convention delegate asked, "Can we forget for whom we are forming a government? Is it for men, or for the imaginary beings called States?"[2] Hamilton identified equal representation of the states in the previous national government as one of the worst defects of the Articles of Confederation. He wrote in Federalist Paper No. 22 that aligning representatives on the basis of statehood rather than population "contradicts the fundamental maxim of republican government, which requires that the sense of the majority should prevail." The larger states, he concluded, "would after a while revolt from the idea of receiving the law from the smaller."[3] Hamilton stated at the Convention, "As states are a collection of individual men, which ought we to respect most: the rights of the people composing them, or the artificial beings resulting from the composition? Nothing could be more preposterous or absurd than to sacrifice the former to the latter."[4]

Like the proposals for the Electoral College, the Framers proposed and debated numerous methods for electing the Senate, none of them satisfying. The "large state versus little state" controversy over whether to grant equal representation per state, regardless of population, threatened to fragment the Constitutional Convention and the formation of the new nation. Prominent among "equal representation" proponents were low-population slave states, where slaves were counted as only three-fifths of a person. The tense negotiations, conducted amid threats of walkouts, with Delaware even threatening to ally itself with another nation if not granted equal representation, resulted in the Great Compromise: the House would be directly elected by the people every two years with representation based on population, and senators would be chosen not by the people but by state legislatures, and for six years with two senators elected per state regardless of population. By design, the senators were to be less responsive to popular sentiment and more sensitive to the needs of property holders, which was especially important to the slave-holding states.[5]

Scanning the course of American history, we can see that Madison and Hamilton were correct in their fears about the antimajoritarian nature of the Senate. For example, equal representation in the Senate perpetuated slavery for decades. Between 1800 and 1860, eight antislavery measures passed the House, only to be killed in the Senate.[6] It took a bloody, fratricidal civil war to resolve what an unrepresentative Senate could not. After the Civil War, southern senators representing low-population ex-slave states continued to wield disproportionate power, using their veto to end Reconstruction and initiate the ugly national scar of brutally racist Jim Crow laws. And then for another century, southern senators blocked the country from enacting federal laws to protect the most basic human rights of African Americans. Other vulnerable constituencies similarly were abandoned by the Senate, such as migrant farmworkers, who were left out of the protections of the National Labor Relations Act in 1935 to win the support of conservative "Boll Weevil" Democratic senators in the South, who did not want to extend federal protections to black farmworkers. So the considerable warts of the Senate's structure have been with us since the beginning.

Let's be clear: Like the Electoral College, the Great Compromise that created the Senate installed antidemocratic and antimajoritarian defects into our constitutional framework. The Senate was not a product of the Framers' brilliant political theory or design. It was merely another improvisation for the sake of expediency, a compromise of principle as the price for gaining a nation. Given how controversial the malapportionment scheme of the Senate was among the Framers, it's surprising how little critique has been focused on the Senate down the centuries. Two researchers who recently completed a major study of the Senate commented, "Journalists, legal scholars, and political scientists have generally ignored the consequences of equal representation of states in the Senate."[7] That's unfortunate because malapportionment in the Senate has resulted in a legislative chamber that has caused considerable damage, making the U.S. government less responsive to the American public.

MICROMINORITY RULE

Nearly a third of the U.S. population now lives in four states— California, Texas, New York, and Florida—which also happen to be four of our most racially diverse states. Yet they are represented by only 8 out of 100 senators. At the same time, 7 percent of the total U.S. population lives in the 17 least populated, mostly lily-white states and is represented by 34 senators, sufficient to kill any treaties or constitutional amendments.[8] California, with 70 times the population of Wyoming, has the same representation in the Senate. Texas, with 22 million people, has the same representation as Montana, with fewer than 1 million people. A senator in Rhode Island represents 500,000 residents, while a senator in New York represents over 9.5 million. Today half of the Senate could be elected by 15 percent of the American people.[9] By filibustering, 41 senators representing little more than one-tenth of the nation can block reforms supported by the other 90 percent.[10]

The alarming trajectory is toward one of ever more flagrant microminority rule. If you think of each state as a senatorial "district," then the districts are nowhere near equal in population or equal in per capita representation as required by the "one person, one vote" principle. In fact, in the High Court's *Reynolds* decision establishing that legal principle, the lone dissenting justice pointed out it meant the Senate was constitutionally suspect, as the 50 states had anything but "substantially equal populations." That contradiction was swept under the carpet where it still lurks, uncomfortably. Consequently, we are facing demographic changes that our 200-year-old senatorial structure is ill prepared to handle.

Conspicuously, if the Senate were chosen by lottery among all Americans, more than a quarter of senators likely would be black or Latino, and more than half would be women. But with two senators elected from each state using the antiquated winner-take-all method, only 6 are minority and 14 women. No, the Senate stands out rather ridiculously, like a bikini at the North Pole, because if it were a private club, a member would need to *resign* before running for public office to avoid charges of belonging to an exclusive fraternity. The U.S. Senate is in the running for the least representative body among Western democracies outside the aristocratic, unelected British House of Lords (which is in the process of being overhauled).

In their groundbreaking work, *Sizing Up the Senate: The Unequal Consequences of Equal Representation*, political scientists Francis Lee and Bruce Oppenheimer demonstrate that the Senate's unique malapportionment scheme profoundly distorts national majorities—policy as well as representation—with severe consequences. According to their research, because low-population states tend to be rural, their senators tend to lean conservative (i.e., Republican). The result is that the Senate's "equal state representation" has overrepresented the Republican Party in every election since 1958, primarily due to Republican success in low-population states in the West and South.[11] More than 200 million votes were cast in races choosing the current 100 senators. Republicans won only 46.8 percent of the votes in these elections—not very close to a majority—and the Democrats won more votes, 48.4 percent. Yet, the GOP currently holds a lopsided 55-to-44 majority. In 2004, over 51 percent of votes cast were for Democratic senatorial candidates, yet Republicans elected 19 of the 34 contested seats (56 percent).[12] Bush carried 31 of 50 states in 2004, most by wide margins, illustrating the GOP advantage in winning a Senate majority when each state has two senators. This 18th-century structural bias so heavily favors Republicans that it's like having a foot race where one side begins 10 steps ahead of the other.

But these revelations turn positively explosive when you compare Senate representation with "Per Capita Tax Burden" tables, ranked by state. Those tables show that Democratic states such as California, New York, Illinois, Massachusetts, and Michigan heavily subsidize GOP states such as Alabama, Mississippi, Alaska, North Dakota, South Dakota, and Oklahoma. Conservatives all across the United States like to shake their fists and inveigh against the evils of big government, high taxes, out-of-control spending, and wasteful programs for minorities. Yet Alaskans receive from the federal government $1.82 for every dollar they pay in federal taxes. Mississippians receive $1.84, North Dakotans $2.03, and West Virginians $1.74 for every federal tax dollar they pay. California, with large urban areas and some of the neediest of residents, receives only $0.81, much less than half of North Dakota and Mississippi. Likewise, New Yorkers receive only $0.81 for every dollar they pay out, and Illinois receives even less, a mere $0.77, just over a third of what North Dakotans receive.[13]

In short, blue state tax dollars end up in red state pockets. It turns out that the most conservative states benefit disproportionately from the types of redistributive government programs that most conservatives usually find so distasteful. Lee and Oppenheimer conclude, "The over-representation of the citizens of the least populous states means that they receive more program funds per capita from the federal government than the citizens of the most populous states. One unanticipated consequence of the Great Compromise, then, is that it now creates a situation in which citizens are treated differently based on where they happen to reside."[14]

Differential treatment based on where one lives is a recurring theme in our 18th-century political system. But it's not just federal appropriations that are affected by the malapportioned Senate. In recent years, conservative senators representing a small segment of the nation have slowed down or thwarted desegregation of schools, campaign finance reform, health care reform, affirmative action, gun control, even basketball programs for inner-city youth. Assistance for cities has been bottled up by senators representing conservative low-population rural states; Bill Clinton's domestic stimulus program, which was targeted at cities in high-population states, was killed by conservative senators from underpopulated states such as Oklahoma. A bill that would have prohibited permanent replacement of strikers passed the House but could not muster the 60 votes necessary to break a Republican filibuster in the Senate.[15] The Senate's power to confirm the president's appointments has allowed this thoroughly unrepresentative body to have a powerful influence on all three branches of government. This speaks volumes about why the U.S. Supreme Court has been so conservative for the past quarter century. In 1991, the 52 senators confirming Clarence Thomas for a lifetime appointment to the Supreme Court represented only 48.6 percent of the nation's population, seven million fewer people than the senators who voted against Thomas. A body as unrepresentative as the Senate should not be confirming these critical appointments, especially not for a life term, and especially not by a simple majority vote.

TIME TO REFORM THE SENATE

Some degree of unequal representation exists in most bicameral legislatures around the world (though not in the 49 American states with bicameral state legislatures, which legally must conform to the "one person, one vote" principle). Yet the degree of unequal representation in the U.S. Senate is by far one of the most extreme. It is time again to ask a fundamental question: Why do people in low-population states deserve special treatment, not only in the Senate but in the Electoral College? Why are they entitled to protection from the will of the national majority?

Can this special 18th-century protection be justified in the 21st century, considering that some of our poorest and most vulnerable citizens live in inner cities of high-population states? Is state-based geography really the best foundation for bestowing special rights and constitutional privilege?

In answering these questions, we should not feel too tightly bound to tradition or history. After all, the Framers first elected the Senate by state legislatures instead of by direct popular vote, eventually leading to a reform movement that culminated in the Seventeenth Amendment in 1916 for direct election of senators. It's past time to reconsider this other bizarre feature that we inherited over the objections of Madison and Hamilton: a malapportioned Senate resulting from affirmative action quotas for low-population states. Nor should we allow the debate to get snagged in the usual partisan trench warfare. This is not an issue of conservatives versus liberals or Democrats versus Republicans—it's an issue of fairness and what's best for the national interest. It wasn't that long ago that populist Democratic senators such as Frank Church (Idaho), Mike Mansfield (Montana), and Henry "Scoop" Jackson (Washington) wielded mighty legislative hammers that benefited their low-population states and the Democratic Party.

Reforming this 18th-century holdover will not be easy because, like the Electoral College, the low-population states that most benefit from its structure have a near-veto over any constitutional amendments, which require support from two-thirds of the Senate and three-fourths of the state legislatures. In addition, Article V of the U.S. Constitution says, "No State, without its Consent, shall be deprived of its equal suffrage in the Senate." And Article IV, Section 3, provides that no state can "be formed by the Junction of two or more States, or parts of States, without the Consent of the Legislatures of the States concerned as well as of the Congress." Not one, but two poison pill provisions. Those slave owners were shrewd, holding Madison and Hamilton over a barrel to exact ironclad constitutional guarantees.

So what will drive reform? The answer is simple: Demographics. The U.S. Senate and the Electoral College are ticking time bombs, demographically speaking. Spanish surnames are increasing five times faster than the general population as the diversity of our nation gallops forward. According to the Census Bureau, by 2025 our four largest states, California, Texas, New York, and Florida, will no longer have a white majority, and they will hold well over a third of the nation's population—yet they will have the same representation in the U.S. Senate as Wyoming, North Dakota, South Dakota, and Alaska, which will hold less than 1 percent of the nation's population.[16] As our nation evolves toward a multiracial amalgam without historical precedent, the built-in representation quotas for low-population, conservative, and predominantly white states in both the Electoral College and the Senate point inevitably toward a future clash. Already African Americans and Latinos make up only 11 percent of the people in the 26 least populous states constituting a Senate majority, though they are 30 percent of the population in the 9 largest states holding a majority of people yet only 18 Senate seats.[17] The gap is widening with each passing year, and increasingly these unrepresentative bodies dominated by white rural America will distort national majorities and push government further out of touch with the multiracial mainstream. The antiquated, antidemocratic defects of the Senate and Electoral College will become too great to ignore, just as Hamilton and Madison warned.

At some point, American government will fall into a phase plagued by a severe legitimacy crisis, much as it did in the mid–19th century. The blue states will adopt an insurrectionary attitude toward the red states regarding their tax and representation subsidies, leading to a resurgence in regional conflict. The racial dimensions of distorted representation in the Senate and Electoral College will warp policy and erode our sense of national unity. Whenever that combination of region, race, culture, and partisanship have collided in American politics, the result

113

usually has been explosive. As this situation tears at the fabric of the nation, even the small-state defenders of the current structure will gradually realize that the status quo is no longer in their interest or the national interest. Momentum for constitutional change will accelerate.

With significant reform of the Senate slowly appearing on the horizon, the question is, What kind of reform will be best? There are halfway solutions and full-blown ones. Halfway solutions, which might be more acceptable at first, would involve greatly reducing the powers of the Senate. Typically, upper chambers have less power than lower chambers, often with little legislative sovereignty other than to delay but not amend or defeat legislation coming from the lower chamber. But the U.S. Senate is the most powerful upper chamber in the world, with more enumerated powers than the House of Representatives, a model that no other nation has copied. Keep in mind that the Framers of the Constitution intended for the Senate to be more aristocratic and propertied than the House. So until we have democratized our House of Lords, its most important powers, particularly the power to confirm Supreme Court justices, should be turned over to the House.

When enough wind is in the sails to fundamentally overhaul the Senate, we have two possibilities: either make the Senate more representative, or abolish the upper chamber entirely. The first option might find the most acceptance. It would give additional senators to the higher-population states and render representation in the Senate closer to "one person, one vote." There may be some convincing arguments for maintaining a degree of representation subsidy for low-population rural areas—and perhaps our poorest citizens living in urban areas as well—but one that is less distorting of national majorities than what the Framers stuck us with. It would not be hard to work out an apportionment formula, based partly on population and partly on need, that could be reviewed every decade or two, providing

fairer, more proportionate representation to all the various interests and constituencies. For instance, each state could be allo-
cated two senators (like they have now) plus one additional
senator for each two million in population. Using this formula,
Wyoming still would have 2 senators, but California as our most
populous state would have 19. California still would have less per
capita representation than Wyoming, but the inequality would
not be as severe. This would increase the size of the Senate perhaps to 190, a workable size.

A more fundamental reform has been proposed by some:
abolishing the upper chamber. This move may not be as radical
as it sounds. Not long ago Sweden abolished its upper chamber
in favor of a unicameral legislature with very little apparent
downsides. Neighboring Finland also has a unicameral legislature, and both countries are known for their competitive
economies (rated first and third by the World Economic Forum)
as well as their premium social and health benefits.[18] In Britain,
all power is invested in the House of Commons, the House of
Lords being a showroom for aristocracy with advisory powers
only. Closer to home, Nebraska is the only state in the United
States with a unicameral state legislature, and it can hardly be
described as a hotbed of radicalism. Benjamin Franklin, known
for his common sense, was a proponent of a unicameral legislature, saying bicameral was like "putting one horse before a cart
and the other behind it, and whipping them both. If the horses
are of equal strength, the wheels of the cart, like the wheels of
government, will stand still."[19]

It's fast approaching time to reconsider the Senate and
whether this thoroughly 18th-century holdover of political elit-
ism and privilege still has a valid role to play. Perhaps a reformed
version does, but we should not automatically assume it; let the
proponents make their case in the face of increasing signs of ob-
solescence. But a solution will only be arrived at through national dialogue and a deeper understanding of how the current

structure really is hurting our nation. Most legislatures, not only in the United States but around the world, base representation on population and on some semblance of proportional representation—the notion that a legislature should, in some fashion, reflect "the people." This is a noble principle that many popular struggles have fought and died for, and one that the American government claims to be exporting to the Middle East and the rest of the world. But in our own country, ironically, this principle still awaits fulfillment. If there is any hope, it is that the fundamental fairness of reform will carry the day, coupled with a bit of self-interest.

▩ Summary of Recommendations

1. Make the U.S. Senate closer to "one person, one vote" by allocating more senators to high-population states.
2. Reduce the powers of the Senate, especially powers of confirmation of judicial appointments, and give them to the House.
3. Or, abolish the Senate and create a unicameral Congress, such as Nebraska's unicameral state legislature.

7

Reclaim the Airwaves

A vital democracy is composed of more than the institutions and practices that administer elections or elect representative government. It also requires institutions of civil society that *support* representative government, including impartial courts, an egalitarian education system, civil liberties, and more. In particular, a modern democracy requires broad public access to free and fair media as the most effective vehicle for informing the public, encouraging political debate, disseminating information, investigating the truth, and engaging wide segments of society.

Yet the American republic is being threatened by a poorly functioning media system that is failing in its basic duties. Increasing levels of media concentration and ownership by huge, transnational corporations are shrinking the number of outlets as well as the marketplace of ideas. A dwindling number of giant media corporations act as gatekeepers with a veto over which issues and leaders will be heard from, frustrating Americans with an appalling lack of choice and competition in the political realm, even as we are bombarded with choice and competition as consumers. Since September 11, 2001, a new threat has emerged from what can only be termed the "national security media," a disturbing overlap between national security interests and compliance of "embedded journalists" who have willingly censored the news, some of them as covertly hired flaks for the Bush administration. What all this amounts to is nothing less than an alarming debasement of the American media that threatens the vitality of our republic.

CONCENTRATION OF MEDIA OWNERSHIP

The broadcast media, both TV and radio, mostly is governed by federal law and the Federal Communications Commission (FCC). Only federal regulation stands in the way of giant media corporations gobbling up the smaller players and shrinking the field. But for many years the federal regulators haven't been doing their job. By 2000, the U.S. media system was dominated by fewer than 10 transnational conglomerates, including Rupert Murdoch's News Corp., General Electric, Viacom, Time Warner, Disney, Vivendi, and Bertelsmann.[1] These seven companies own a staggering array of media properties, including NBC, CBS, ABC, MTV, CNN, Fox News, Turner Broadcasting, ESPN, America Online, *Time* magazine, and more. In 1990, the major broadcast networks—ABC, CBS, NBC, and Fox—fully or partially owned just 12.5 percent of the new television series they aired; the rest were from independent producers. By 2000, the figure was 56.3 percent. Just two years later, it had surged to 77.5 percent. Ted Turner, founder of CNN and a former media tycoon, has declared, "No one should underestimate the danger. Big media companies want to eliminate all ownership limits."[2]

In the radio sector, consolidation has resulted in over 4,000 commercial radio stations being sold and over 1,000 radio company mergers. Corporate broadcaster Clear Channel has grown from 40 stations nationwide to over 1,200 since the mid-1990s. Viacom and Clear Channel alone control 42 percent of listeners and 45 percent of industry revenue. With fewer players in the radio business, advertising rates have spiked 155 percent in Atlanta and 30 percent in New York, San Diego, and Las Vegas.[3] In addition, programming has become more rigidly controlled and less locally based. Stations owned by a conglomerate often play only canned programming and music, all driven by computer from a distant location. Former FCC chairman William Kennard has said, "I don't think anybody anticipated that the pace would be so fast and so dramatic. The fundamental economic structure of the radio industry is changing from one of independently owned operators to something akin to a chain store."[4]

Thus, a controversial decision in June 2003 by the FCC to lift the already-too-low caps on the allowable levels of media concentration and ownership of TV and radio was viewed with great alarm. The vote was strictly partisan: The three Republicans outvoted the two Democrats on the commission. The Republican chairman of the FCC who spearheaded the effort was Michael Powell, son of then-secretary of state Colin Powell.

The FCC ruling was just the latest of a longer arc of corporate and conservative attempts to concentrate the media in fewer and fewer hands. The Telecommunications Act of 1996 deregulated the telecommunications industry and made takeovers and mergers even easier by raising the percentage of national broadcast audience that may be controlled by one entity, from 25 percent to 35 percent. This resulted in a land rush of mergers among national television and radio broadcasters. The 2003 FCC ruling sought to further accelerate this trend by raising the national audience caps to 45 percent from 35 percent.[5] Ted Turner weighed in against this move by the FCC, writing in a widely circulated opinion piece, "With the removal of these limits, immense media power will pass into the hands of a very few corporations and individuals."[6]

American democracy dodged that bullet when a federal appeals court struck down the new FCC rules in June 2004.[7] Still, it seemed only to slow, not stop, the media concentration. Clear Channel has continued its Pac-Man ways, gobbling up smaller stations and adding to the bland homogeneity of commercial radio. And Rupert Murdoch's Fox, General Electric's NBC, and others continue to lobby Congress to rewrite the Telecommunications Act and sweep away limits on the number of media outlets they can control.

Meanwhile, the media monopolists have fought even the smallest encroachment on their turf. In 1999, a different FCC voted to take a step toward democratizing America's airwaves by issuing hundreds of noncommercial, low-power FM radio licenses. So-called microradio stations would have the capacity to broadcast anywhere from 1 to 3.5 miles, an infinitesimally small range compared to the powerful transmitters of commercial stations. The microradio stations were going to be low-tech community stations, both rural and urban, providing programming about local events and themes that the megacommercial stations seeking a larger audience would never provide. And there was evidence of a real need because the media concentration and loss of local content had undercut the public service mission of the media, which in some instances had dangerous consequences. For example, in early 2002 a freight train derailed near Minot, North Dakota, releasing a toxic cloud of anhydrous ammonia over the town. Police tried to alert the public by calling local radio stations, six of which were owned by Clear Channel. It took over an hour to reach anyone at the stations to put an alert on the air because no one was there to answer the phone—the canned programming for all six stations was being beamed from a Clear Channel computer in San Antonio, Texas, 1,600 miles away. By the next day, 300 people had been hospitalized, many partially blinded by the ammonia, and pets and livestock had died.[8]

So the bid for microradio seemed to be an appropriate marriage of Big and Little, enriching the milieu of all. But an unlikely coalition composed of the behemoth corporate lobby National Association of Broadcasters (NAB) and the nonprofit National Public Radio banded together to fight against this FCC decision. It was a real low point for NPR, which was worried that the microradio stations would interfere with its signal, a view the FCC engineers rejected as technically unsound.[9] NAB spent millions lobbying Congress, and with political cover provided by the underfunded and increasingly corporate-sponsored NPR, the FCC decision was effectively bottled up in Congress.[10]

The effects of a media system in fewer and fewer hands have become increasingly apparent. The corporate media pick and choose what to air, and the evidence is overwhelming that their criteria for choosing America's information fare has little to do with the public interest. Saturated by the values of sensationalism, entertainment, and profiteering, there is little room on the corporate dial for the values of political pluralism, stimulating discussion of ideas and issues, information dissemination, or investigative journalism. With 100 channels of laugh tracks, home shopping infomercials, and pay-per-view, the information necessities of a free-thinking society are swallowed up in the unregulated, free-for-all regime dominated by the corporate media.

AGAINST THE PUBLIC INTEREST:
Undermining Political Debate

While steamrolling over Lilliputian, community-based micro-radio, corporate broadcasters benefit from a nearly $400 billion government subsidy that hands over control of the public's airwaves to them for free.[11] When the Communications Act of 1934 granted broadcasters free and exclusive licenses to the public airwaves, it did so on the condition that they agreed "to serve the public interest." So what have the broadcasters done with their commitment to the public interest?

For starters, they have reduced their political coverage. Robert Lichter of the Center for Media and Public Affairs said his organization's study of the 2000 election showed that "two elections ago the three networks together gave you about 25 minutes a night of election news, or about eight minutes apiece. [In the 2000] election they gave you about 12 minutes, or four minutes apiece per night."[12] Of that reduced amount of election news, an average of only 64 seconds per night was quality time with the candidates discussing issues or their views. The rest was "horse race" speculation about who might win the election.[13] In addition, since 1968 the average presidential campaign sound bite on network news had declined from 43 seconds to 8.2 seconds. Gary Ruskin, director of Commercial Alert, commented, "Third graders communicate in longer segments than that."[14] Astoundingly, Lichter discovered that presidential candidate George W. Bush received more airtime in a single guest appearance on the *Late Show with David Letterman* than he received during all of October 2000 on all three network newscasts combined.[15]

Reducing political coverage has meant that, increasingly, politicians in a campaign season have no choice but to buy more television ads. Political TV ads bring in an estimated $1 billion in revenue to broadcasters. Though they only appear for a few months out of the year, political commercials were the third-largest source of TV advertising revenue for broadcasters, trailing only automotive and retail ads.[16] Some media analysts contend that this has led to a brazenly bottom-line move on the part of television broadcasters—decrease political coverage, forcing candidates to buy more TV time. Which would mean that broadcasters are selling back to candidates the airwaves they have been given for free by the public.

Not only that, but the broadcasters are actively *gouging* campaigns during the political season. As Election Day approaches, prices for TV spots typically double and triple, sometimes within hours. One consultant from a firm handling congressional races reported how a Philadelphia station quoted a $900 price for a particular TV slot. "When my buyer called a few hours later to place the ad, she was told, sorry, the price is now up to $1,150." In Portland, Oregon, the Sierra Club found that the price of a 30-second spot more then tripled in less than one month. A Brigham Young University study of 17 hotly contested

U.S. Senate and congressional races in 2000 found that the average cost for all political spots rose from less than $500 in mid-August to more than $1,200 in the final week of the campaign.[17] It is difficult to see how this kind of gouging serves the public interest. Unsurprisingly, the broadcasters have fought any attempts to curtail their billion-dollar cash cow.

The corporate media also have become an arbiter of a candidate's viability. While most races are not competitive due to partisan residential patterns in Red versus Blue America, elections for some of our most important offices can be real cliffhangers. Front-runner candidates are vetted by corporate media gatekeepers, and, in the little political coverage the media bothers with, broadcasters and newspapers routinely ignore certain candidates and exclude them from debates, especially independent and minor party candidates. The media's reasons for these exclusions vary, but particularly in the case of independent and minor party candidates, most often the reason cited is that these candidates are not viable—they can't win. But as we have seen, most legislative races across the country are one-party fiefdoms not competitive for a Democratic or Republican candidate, either. If that truly were the coverage criteria, the media only would cover the obvious winner in each race. But typically only the independent and minor party candidates are ignored, even when those candidates have sound ideas and legitimate credentials.

Disappointingly, public broadcasting has not been much better than the corporate media on this score, excluding political alternatives from campaign debates and coverage. The media's refusal to cover political alternatives should be reasonably viewed as an in-kind *donation*, a reportable independent expenditure, to the Democrats' and Republicans' campaigns. It raises disturbing questions about the cozy relationship between the American media and the Democrats and Republicans, stifling most political dissent and opposition in a way that is not altogether different from the relationship between the old Soviet

Politburo and its Communist propaganda machines. The specter of the media deciding the viability of political candidates—and, by extension, which issues and policies will be discussed during campaigns—should be utterly offensive to a democratic society. The fact that the corporate media feed at the public trough with so little accountability raises this disposition to the level of a national outrage.

THE NATIONAL SECURITY MEDIA

Since September 11, 2001, a new threat to a democratic media has emerged in the form of the "national security media"—an alarming pattern of government manipulation of the media and "embedded journalists" who willingly censor the news or are covertly paid to espouse the government's viewpoint. Going to war and fighting terrorism is serious business, requiring for its execution a great trust between the nation's leaders and the public. National security concerns always will require a degree of control over sensitive information, but since September 11, the public interest has been ill served by the Bush administration's attempts to manipulate the media and the public.

The episodes involving journalists Armstrong Williams and Maggie Gallagher, who were paid by the Bush administration to espouse a conservative viewpoint without disclosing the financial arrangements,[18] were reminiscent of the Office of Public Diplomacy (OPD) established by President Ronald Reagan's CIA director William Casey in the 1980s. The OPD's mission was to affect U.S. public opinion about Reagan's covert war in Central America. It secretly recruited journalists, political scientists, and other intellectuals to place op-eds in the nation's newspapers and to act as news sources espousing the administration's party line. It funneled money into organizations, including right-wing Christian church groups, that promoted the administration's line about Central America. It was a Goebbels-like propaganda arm, pure and simple, that eventually was disbanded after its true nature was publicized.[19]

The case against Williams and Gallagher must be understood in this light. There is a pattern here, amplified in December 2005 when the U.S. military was caught red-handed having secretly paid Iraqi newspapers to print more than 1,000 articles of pro-American propaganda, and covertly paying monthly stipends to Iraqi journalists.[20] *USA Today* reported that the Pentagon launched a $300 million psychological warfare operation run by experts at the U.S. Special Operations Command, including plans for placing pro-American propaganda in foreign media outlets without disclosing the source of the information.[21]

Slightly less obvious than covert government propaganda operations, but nevertheless insidious in its impact on public information, has been the type of "insider" journalism practiced by *New York Times* reporter Judith Miller and the *Washington Post*'s Bob Woodward. Miller in particular misled the country to war by dutifully reporting whatever her anonymous Pentagon and Iraqi exile sources told her about weapons of mass destruction and the like, nearly all of which turned out to be distortions or outright deceptions.[22] Was it Miller's ambition to scoop the headlines or her blind patriotism that caused her to report her sources' fabrications without digging for the truth? We may never know, but her shoddy reporting and that of others contributed tragically to the United States going to war under false pretenses. Miller and the *New York Times* legitimized going to war in a way that the cheerleaders at Fox News never could, because the *Times* was seen as something of an opposition newspaper. This fiasco eventually prompted the *Times*'s editors to issue an unprecedented national apology over its pre–Iraq war coverage. But it was too little too late, and the *Times*'s apology appeared on page A10 instead of on the front page, where many of Miller's discredited stories had appeared.[23]

The failure of the fourth estate was never more evident than during the months-long buildup to the Iraq invasion, when *New York Times* columnist Paul Krugman commented that Europeans and Americans "have different views [of the war] partly because we see different news. At least compared with their foreign counterparts, the 'liberal' U.S. media are strikingly conservative—and in this case hawkish."[24] Fox News spokeswoman Irena Briganti lashed out at CNN's top war correspondent, Christiane Amanpour, for later stating that the press had muzzled itself during the Iraq war and that CNN "was intimidated by the Bush administration and its foot soldiers at Fox News," which cast "a climate of fear and self-censorship." As if on cue, Fox's Briganti responded, "Given the choice, it's better to be viewed as a foot soldier for Bush than a spokeswoman for al Qaeda."[25]

These sorts of nationalist media postures and propaganda efforts, while not unexpected during wartime, must be recognized for what they are: a direct threat to independent media and their watchdog responsibilities. They also are a disturbing reminder of how government influence over the media has been used by rulers throughout history to manipulate public opinion. The *New York Times* recovered somewhat from its earlier capitulations when its investigative reporters broke the news in December 2005 about the president's controversial secret domestic spying operations. But it also was revealed that the *Times* had delayed publishing the story for at least a year, apparently at the government's request. The vulnerability of free speech and dissent in an era of media consolidation and embedded journalism was jarringly displayed when Cumulus Media Inc. and Cox Communications banned the popular country band Dixie Chicks from hundreds of their music stations nationwide for 30 days after lead singer Natalie Maines criticized President Bush for the war in Iraq.

With the near-collapse of the American media in their fulcrum duties of informing the public, investigating the truth, and facilitating healthy public discourse, whether over politics, candidates, or national security, it has become difficult to learn what is happening in the world, or even in the United States, without consulting non-American news sources such as the British Broadcasting Corporation (BBC) or European and other foreign media sources via TV, radio, and the World Wide Web. It's as if someone needs to create a Radio Free America that can beam independent news sources into the United States, ones that are less compromised by national security interests and corporate commercialism. Unsurprisingly, 60 percent of Americans believe that news organizations are "politically biased in their reporting," up from 45 percent in 1985.[26] That opinion is a sad commentary on the state of a multibillion-dollar media industry that benefits from huge public subsidies with little accountability. We are not getting our money's worth.

A DEMOCRATIC FIRST AMENDMENT

As various legal and media experts have pointed out, the classic First Amendment situation of a political dissident sounding off from a street corner soapbox, spouting her or his "free speech," is mostly is mostly a quaint anachronism.[27] Instead, the flow of information, political debate, and influence has been removed from the street corner into our living rooms, automobiles, and workplaces, piped in mostly by huge media conglomerates that have a lot more and a lot louder speech than everyone else. By controlling the medium of communication, they control what is heard and seen. It's as if they have turned up *their* volume and drowned everyone else out. It's not that others can't speak; it's just that we can't hear them. Hence, *effective* political speech today is no longer free; it's quite expensive, and very few can afford it.

Legally speaking, however, a media conglomerate is recognized as a private individual, and judicial interpretation of the First Amendment is blind to any difference between a street corner radical and Rupert Murdoch or CBS. Traditional civil libertarian defenses of the First Amendment make forceful anticensorship arguments for the political dissident's right to speak out without being censored by the government; it is a principle that the United States has exported around the world, whether speaking against Communist governments' censorship of Andrei Sakharov and Solidarity labor activists or South Africa's jailing of Nelson Mandela. But with corporate media conglomerates treated as "individuals," anticensorship arguments have created a communications marketplace stripped of crucial government regulations. Applied to the "individual autonomy" rights of each corporate media outlet, anticensorship policies have become the opposite of antitrust policies, fostering a deregulated ocean of "media free trade" where the big gobble the little.

For example, the media corporations that lobbied the FCC in 2003 to lift the ownership caps from 35 percent to 45 percent used anticensorship arguments to make their case. They viewed ownership caps as a violation of their individual right to own as much "free speech" as they can afford. Anticensorship arguments were used to lobby for the dreadful Telecommunications Act of 1996. The Turner Broadcasting System used an anticensorship argument in its case against a 1992 federal law that required cable systems to set aside up to one-third of their channels for local broadcasts.[28] Turner Broadcasting claimed that such set-asides censored its individual First Amendment right to select who could speak on its cable station. Anticensorship arguments have been used to fight set-asides for minority-owned businesses of frequencies for cellular communication services, to fight campaign finance reform laws and restrictions on commercial speech and advertising, and to sue "truth in advertising" laws that prohibit political campaigns from knowingly making false statements.

Thus, anticensorship policies have been misused to allow the wealthiest interests to grab bigger and bigger chunks of the media market. Those with the most individual autonomy (i.e., money) naturally have ended up with the most speech. In the modern era of corporate speech and the mass media, increasingly the "individual autonomy" paradigm and anticensorship arguments not only are anachronisms but are undermining attempts to create a more democratic media. For if the government isn't allowed to regulate the behavior of powerful corporations, media or otherwise, who can? The times call for a new, more democratic conception of the First Amendment that will help us corral the corporate media.

A better legal foundation for the First Amendment should be to enhance—in the words of free speech champion Justice William Brennan—a "robust public debate" of issues. The "robust debate" principle recognizes that sometimes in a crowd of speakers, it is necessary to turn down the volume of certain loud and clamorous speakers (e.g., NBC, CBS, Rupert Murdoch) in order to give others a chance to speak. Or, at the very least, it's necessary to turn up the volume of others who can't be heard, with government regulation and subsidies used to foster this public good. A paradigm shift like this has huge ramifications for democratic discourse. A "robust public debate" principle for the First Amendment would give us the legal tool for democratizing our media. As we search for solutions, we should advance ones that enhance the robust debate principle and steer away from applying civil libertarian–type anticensorship/individual autonomy arguments to the corporate media. Size matters in an age of mass communication, and there needs to be a different set of rules and laws for the big players that recognizes the realities of the media landscape and the needs of a democratic society.

STEPS TO RECLAIM THE AIRWAVES

With an overarching strategy of promoting the robust debate principle of the First Amendment, one of the first steps in reclaiming the public's airwaves is to prevent further media consolidation. Ted Turner, founder of CNN, says media companies

have grown so large and powerful, and their dominance has become so detrimental to the survival of small, emerging media
companies (such as a young CNN), that only one alternative remains: bust up the big conglomerates. "We've done this before,"
says Turner, "to the railroad monopolies in the first part of the
twentieth century, to phone companies more recently."[29] If we
can't use antitrust laws to break up the conglomerates, at the
very least we must prevent them from growing any larger and
prevent the FCC or Congress from passing any regulations that
permit more consolidation.

Antitrust oversight also should be applied to the cable TV
industry. The cable TV industry has a long history of anticom-
petitive practices. According to the Center for Digital Democracy, companies such as Comcast and Time Warner now control
access to the majority of TV channels available to the 7 out of 10
U.S. households that subscribe to cable television. It's become
almost impossible for independent programmers and alternative
channels to gain entry because cable giants have often forced
competing programmers to cede them control or ownership
stake in their ventures as a condition of access to the cable channels. It is imperative that Congress better regulate the cable industry to open it up to more competition and to make sure that
it serves the public interest.

We also must restore the Fairness Doctrine, which for many
years required broadcasters to offer a range of opinions about
significant public issues. But the Fairness Doctrine was created
by an FCC regulation, not a federal law, and the Reagan administration gutted it in the 1980s, robbing the public of badly
needed opportunities to hear from a range of viewpoints.[30]
That's when the country began experiencing a proliferation of
highly partisan news outlets that disseminate unbalanced news
coverage, and talk radio and Rush Limbaugh Land were born,
followed by Fox News. It's clear that abolishing the Fairness
Doctrine has led to an impoverished public discourse where too
many media consumers are bunkered down in their own partisan

media ghettos, tuned in to a narrow world that reinforces their own and rarely challenged by other viewpoints. Representative Louise Slaughter of New York and others are working to reestablish balance to broadcasting by passing a federal law to restore the Fairness Doctrine.

But the most fundamental media reform requires establishing a more robust and well-funded public broadcasting sector. A dynamic public TV and radio sector on the order of the BBC is really the most effective counterbalance to the market-driven corporate media. American public television is badly underfunded, with an annual budget that amounts to about $3 per capita—compared with $25 in Canada and over $50 in Sweden, Germany, and Britain.[31] Nearly as important as the level of funding is the mechanism of public funding. In the United States, public broadcasting is funded by budget allocations from a hostile right-wing Congress and corporations. Its survival—and therefore its independence—is always in doubt, and, unsurprisingly, an internal audit revealed that National Public Radio is tap dancing to the tune of its funders—63 percent of think tank talking heads interviewed in 2005 by NPR were conservative, only 37 percent liberal, nearly a 2-to-1 ratio.[32]

Instead of funding from politically manipulable budget allocations, the BBC is funded by mandatory public subscription fees where all households are required to pay a monthly amount of approximately $25 (like the monthly cable TV fee many Americans pay). This gives the BBC its own funding base substantially independent of the government. The BBC also is guided by a public charter that spells out in detail its public obligations (unlike the American corporate media's vague promise "to serve the public interest"). The BBC's charter provides requirements and guidelines for editorial standards, impartiality, "disseminating information, education and entertainment," "fair and informed debate at local, regional and national levels," "programmes of an educational nature" including for children and young people, and much more.[33] The BBC's independent funding base combined with its prescriptive charter is what allows it to display a level of journalistic independence from the government as well as programming variety and quality that American broadcasting, whether public or private, can only fantasize about. Germany and Sweden's public broadcasting sectors also are funded by household monthly subscription fees and serve their publics according to precisely enumerated charters.

Europeans do another smart thing that fosters a more robust debate of ideas—they subsidize daily newspapers and magazines. That's why you see European news racks bursting with so many colorful magazines and newspapers, with political orientations from the right to the left to the center and back again. Not only does this variety encourage political pluralism and ideas, but it encourages a higher level of newspaper readership than in the United States, and further reduces dependence on commercial television.[34] But in the United States, we have experienced extreme consolidation in the newspaper industry, just like in the radio and TV industries. This has resulted in major cities either with a single daily newspaper owned by a large newspaper chain, or with joint operating agreements among supposedly competing dailies that increasingly look like carbon copies. Locally owned dailies have nearly disappeared, and many small and midsized towns have no local newspaper at all.

Fewer newspapers have contributed to a decline in newspaper readership across the United States, which is not some academic matter. Studies have demonstrated that newspapers are more informative than television, and newspaper readers retain more information than TV viewers. A wider level of newspaper and magazine readership contributes not only to greater literacy among the general population but also to a greater degree of what political scientist Henry Milner has called "civic literacy"—more citizens who are informed and conversant in the politics and issues of the day.[35] Thus, boosting newspaper readership is key to maintaining an engaged citizenry as well as some degree of local focus. Public subsidies of daily newspapers and magazines would lead to a flowering of print media fare across the nation that appeals to more Americans and promotes literacy as well as civic literacy. Daily newspaper reading in elementary and high school classrooms would get students into the habit of reading the news. Interestingly, American media analyst Robert McChesney says that "Madison and Jefferson were big believers in massive subsidies to spawn a print media that never would have existed if left to the market. That's why we had a huge postal subsidy, and massive subsidies of our media at the very beginning of the republic."[36]

We also should return control of the public's airwaves to the public. The government has been a terrible caretaker of our commonwealth as established by the Communications Act of 1934. Government should regulate the corporate media to ensure that in return for receiving free access to nearly $400 billion worth of the public's airwaves, they are serving the legally mandated public interest. That public interest should be defined by a more detailed BBC-like charter that at the very least provides free media time for political candidates, televised political debates in which multiple points of view are included, more and better news coverage (instead of "if it bleeds it leads" headline news), set-asides for local channels and minority points of view, and support for microradio and public cable access TV. Corporate broadcasters should have to sign on the dotted line and agree to detailed provisions stipulating the ways they will serve the public interest in order to receive their free access to the public's airwaves.

It is also crucial that steps be taken right away to protect and expand community broadband Internet access. Broadband Internet access has replaced dial-up as the preferred means of reaching the Internet. It provides a faster and more stable connection that enables better use of streaming technology, videos on the Web, and more. But under the commercial control of cable and local telephone companies, such connections remain beyond the financial means of many households. The United States lags far behind Europe—even behind poor countries such as Estonia—in terms of wireless and broadband availability.[37]

In response, towns and cities across the United States have begun doing a very smart thing: building their own high-speed networks to create affordable Internet access. But the big commercial broadband providers, rather than figuring out how to work with these communities' efforts, decided they threaten their profits. So they have begun lobbying government to halt these community networks. In the highest-profile case to date, Verizon and Comcast successfully lobbied the Pennsylvania state legislature to bar all cities and towns in Pennsylvania from offering Internet access to consumers. After protests from Philadelphia, which already had taken steps to create affordable citywide broadband access, Democratic governor Ed Rendell signed a version of the bill that exempted Philadelphia, but the rest of the state got shafted.[38] Efforts to produce affordable broadband access will be critical over the next decade.

Many battles lie ahead to reclaim the American media and make it into one that facilitates the type of robust public debate that a modern democracy requires. What is at stake is nothing less than a choice between a communications environment that reflects the highest aspirations of a democratic culture, including access, diversity, meaningful public discourse, broad information dissemination, an informed citizenry, balanced news coverage, and journalistic integrity, or one that has been swallowed by the dictates of corporate commercialism and national security.

■ Summary of Recommendations

1. Stop media consolidation—use antitrust laws to break up the media conglomerates.
2. Break up the cable TV monopoly.
3. Restore the Fairness Doctrine.

4. Establish a more robust public broadcasting sector (TV and radio) to counterbalance the corporate media.
5. Subsidize daily newspapers and magazines; increase "civic literacy;" establish daily newspaper reading in classrooms to get students into the habit of reading the news.
6. Return the airwaves to the public—with free media time for candidates, televised political debates, more political news and balanced coverage, minority set-asides, support of microradio, and public cable access TV.
7. Protect and expand community broadband Internet access.

■ Organizations to Contact

Free Press, **http://freepress.net**, (866) 666-1533

MuniWireless.com (reports on community wireless and broadband projects)

Media Channel, **www.mediachannel.org**, (212) 246-0202

Center for Media and Democracy, **www.prwatch.org**, (608) 260-9713

Center for Digital Democracy, **www.democraticmedia.org**, (202) 986-2220

Media Alliance, **www.media-alliance.org**, (510) 832-9000

Reclaim the Media, **www.reclaimthemedia.org**

Independent World Television, **www.iwtnews.com**

Link TV, **www.worldlinktv.org**

8

Minimize Money's Role

One of the most discussed political reforms over the last 30 years has been campaign finance reform. That reform effort blames much of what ails our representative democracy on the pernicious effect of private money in politics. In the 1990s, tales of the Keating Five, Lincoln Bedroom, and Buddhist temples became the stuff of political legend. More recently, House majority leader Tom DeLay was accused of campaign and money-laundering violations, lobbyist Jack Abramoff pled guilty to influence peddling and bribery of various congressional members, and big GOP donors such as Halliburton were awarded sweetheart government contracts. The 2004 presidential candidates set new records by spending $1.7 billion, nearly twice the amount spent in 2000.[1] Such stories have created a widespread perception of cronyism, corruption, and a "pay to play" political system swamped with money.

Beneath this perception is an irrefutable fact: It now takes a lot of money to run for office. Besides the soaring costs of a presidential campaign, a single congressional district today has about 650,000 residents, and a state senate district in California has 850,000 residents. Without access to gobs of money for TV and radio ads, direct mail, and other ways of broadcasting to the public, underfunded and non-media-sanctioned candidates have little means to connect with voters. In many races, sometimes only one candidate per race has access to those kinds of resources. The 2004 presidential election was a contest between, in the words of Fox News commentator Bill O'Reilly, "two silver spooners."[2] As a result, voters do not hear a range of viewpoints. Vigorous debate vanishes among the expensive, poll-driven, sound bite campaigns, and voters and democracy are the losers.

This loss of political debate and new ideas is one of the most insidious downsides to our privately financed campaigns. That's why I was one of the organizers (along with Common Cause and Democracy Matters) of efforts to pass legislation in both San Francisco and Oakland for public financing of local races. I believe strongly in public financing of campaigns as one of the essential reforms needed to repair our broken democracy. This is particularly true since the U.S. Supreme Court in the mid-1970s ruled that candidate spending caps and most restrictions of campaign funding (other than limits on the amount of individual donations to candidates) are unconstitutional.[3] It was one of the worst decisions the High Court ever rendered, and it has greatly limited reform possibilities. Some legal experts have hope that the Supreme Court may modify their opinion in the near future, but I'm not optimistic. Given the legal constraints, public financing is the most promising campaign finance reform because it helps level the playing field by providing all candidates with sufficient resources to communicate with voters, and it provides incentives for candidates to voluntarily accept spending limits.

Yet it often bothers me that some of my reform colleagues have oversold the significance of campaign finance reform. We frequently hear that campaign finance reform—whether public financing, donation limits, free airtime, or spending caps—will lead to greater competition in our elections, wash candidates "clean" from the effects of money, and change election outcomes as well as legislative policy. One organization even proclaimed, "Getting private money out of public elections is the unfinished business of the voting rights movement," implying that doing so will elect significantly more minority representatives—a claim that is demonstrably false.

After more than 30 years of campaign finance reform, including the use of public financing of campaigns in several states, the presidential election, and a host of municipal elections, I see little evidence that these claims are accurate. I wish that were not the case; I wish that campaign finance reform was the magic bullet some say it is, "the reform that makes all other reforms possible," as some have called it. But the truth is, it's not—at least, not by itself. Where reforms have been passed, particularly public financing of campaigns, there is solid evidence of more contested races and candidates representing more points of view. That in turn has increased political debate, information for voters, and engagement of voters—a great accomplishment. But there is little evidence that more *contested* races have led to more *competitive* races, an important distinction. In fact, at least one state with public financing of campaigns has seen a decrease in electoral competition.

What's needed now, I believe, is a new and more effective approach to campaign finance reform. In particular, we need to see why campaign finance reform, particularly public financing of elections and free media access, is a necessary but insufficient step toward repairing our democracy.

THE HYPE OF REFORMERS

Each election cycle—you can set your calendar by it—leading campaign finance reform organizations issue a postelection press release announcing something like "Money Wins Big, Top Spenders Capture 9 Out of 10 Races." One headline from a report blared "Money Largely Determines Election Outcomes."[4] These announcements declare that getting private money out of campaigns, or at least reducing spending inequities between candidates, will significantly affect American politics.

But as we have seen in previous chapters, campaign spending inequities are not the cause of the many lopsided one-party districts in the United States today. Those are produced by partisan residential patterns in Red and Blue America combined with district-based, winner-take-all elections. Sure, the winners have more money than challengers, but what's the cause and what's the effect? The money goes to candidates who donors *know* will win, because the partisan demographics of the district guarantee that result. By betting on the sure horse in each race, donors hope they're buying access and influence—not elections. In other words, for most elections, money follows electoral success, not vice versa. But by reversing cause and effect, these headlines confuse our understanding of how our democracy works and how to repair it. And that confusion exaggerates our expectations of how much campaign finance reform really can accomplish, leading to disappointment among reformers, the public, and funders of reform.

That realization was never clearer than in May 2005, when I addressed the annual convention of the Arizona League of Women Voters. Spearheaded by the League in 1998 and 2000, Arizona had enacted two of the most talked-about reforms: full public financing of campaigns for state elections, and a nonpartisan independent redistricting commission. Arizona's reform success created excitement and hope across the nation. Yet I found the League of Women Voters, as well as other Arizona reformers, downright glum about their efforts. Apparently the recent electoral results hadn't matched their expectations or their campaign hype. In fact, the Grand Canyon State had seen some of the least competitive races in the nation in 2004. None of the 30 state senate seats was competitive, and more than half of the seats were uncontested by one of the two major parties. In the state house, which uses two-seat districts, half the races were uncontested by a major party, and only 5 out of 60 races were competitive. In the end, 97 percent of incumbents won reelection, whether their campaigns were publicly financed or privately financed (and despite having an independent redistricting commission removing the worst excesses of incumbent gerrymandering).

Those are not the results one would hope for in a state that has been at the forefront of political reform. To be sure, some positives have occurred in Arizona as well—for example, a decent increase in the number of candidates running in the primaries and for statewide executive offices, which fostered more political debate. And 10 of the 11 winners for statewide office were publicly financed candidates, including current governor Janet Napolitano. But, on the other hand, the number of women candidates in the primaries declined steadily from 71 in 2000 to 66 in 2002 to 59 in 2004, only 29 percent of primary candidates; and the number of minority candidates, after increasing significantly from 13 in 2000 to 37 in 2002, decreased to 34 in 2004, only 17 percent of all primary candidates (in a state that is 36 percent minority).[5] And there has been no noticeable impact on legislative policy.

In Maine, another state with full public financing of campaigns, results have been somewhat better but still not earth-shattering. On the positive side, the number of contested primaries rose to 39 in 2004, up from 25 in 2000, fostering more political debate (though that's out of 186 races, still a small fraction overall). And in the November election, only two races were uncontested by a major party in the state senate, and seven in the house. At least three independent legislators' victories can be attributed partly to public financing allowing them to knock off candidates of both major parties.[6] But Maine also remains dogged by mostly noncompetitive elections: In 2004, the average victory margin for 35 state senate races and 151 state house races was a landslide of 20 points. Only four races in the senate were highly competitive (won by less than five points), while 31 in the house were, the latter a decent showing. But twice as many house races, 62 overall, were won by huge landslide margins. And the number of women in the Maine Legislature has dropped to its lowest level in 20 years. One report examining public financing in Maine, Arizona, and elsewhere concluded "there is little evidence that public funding has increased representation of women . . . or the number of women who run for office."[7]

So after all their hard work, it was not surprising that Arizona reformers expressed disappointment. Ever an optimist, I told the reformers to take heart: It's not that public financing and independent redistricting commissions aren't good reforms; it's just that they are more limited in their impact than most people realize. In Arizona, as in many states, public financing (and redistricting commissions) are made less potent by the red and blue partisan residential patterns combined with the winner-take-all electoral system. Over the past 15 years, liberals and Democrats have become more numerous in the southern part of the state (around Tucson), while conservatives and Republicans dominate the rest of the state. The only way to make winner-take-all districts more competitive would be to draw narrow bands that extend vertically from south to north, like the teeth of a fork. However, such districts not only would look ridiculous but also would break up communities of interest, such as geographic regions and racial minorities, showing the trade-off of winner-take-all districts—you can have competitive elections or representative results, but it's pretty difficult to have both. Unfortunately, there's little that publicly financed elections, or even redistricting commissions, can do to counter these realities. Demography in Arizona—like in so many other states—has become destiny.

Public financing's greatest successes have been realized in city elections, such as New York City and Los Angeles, which use public financing for mayor, city council, and other races. There, we see strong evidence that the availability of public funds has helped level the playing field and produced more minority and women candidates, especially for leading offices such as mayor and city council. More minority candidates also seem to have produced more engagement on the part of minority communities. Los Angeles's current Latino mayor was a publicly funded candidate, and, as of 2002, approximately half the members of the New York City Council were minorities and a quarter were women, most of whom received public financing (on the other hand, most of these cities' council races were completely noncompetitive).[8] But these cities are heavily Democratic, so elections are fought along different battle lines than the red and blue fiefdoms of state and federal politics.

In short, Arizona and other states finds themselves in situations where the problem is not simply whether one candidate greatly outspends the other. The problem also is balkanized partisan residential patterns combined with electing legislators via a checkerboard electoral map of individual districts. Campaign finance reform is valuable but insufficient. I told the Arizona reformers that it was time to take the next step, which is to scrap their winner-take-all system and start using proportional representation along with public financing of campaigns—a powerful combination that would greatly increase competition and substantially improve representative government in Arizona.

THE PUZZLE OF QUID PRO QUO

Rather than the level of political competition, some campaign finance reformers focus on the quid pro quo between politicians and donors—the granting of legislative favors in return for big donations from lobbyists and influence peddlers like Jack Abramoff and his ilk. There is a belief that public financing of campaigns, even in the face of an avalanche of noncompetitive safe seats, will make the politicians act differently because they won't need to rely on special interests to raise money, and so this change in association will also affect their votes. I believe there is much truth to this view, but a key question is, How much? To what degree does *who* politicians raise money from affect overall policy, especially in major policy areas?

When you look at the amount of political donations from corporations and various industries, although obviously it is a lot of money by the standard of the average voter, it is really a small amount for these corporations. For instance, a leading campaign finance reform newsletter called *OUCH! A Regular Bulletin on How Money in Politics Hurts You*, reported that the senators who voted against an amendment to bankruptcy legislation received $34,520 more on average from the banking and credit industry than the senators who voted in favor of the amendment, the implication being that the donations affected their votes. But that was over a six-year period, which works out to less than $6,000 per senator per year.[9] Apparently a senator can be bought pretty cheaply. It also implies that for a mere $6,000 per year the supporters of the amendment could *buy back* those senators' votes, which is clearly incorrect. One can point to numerous examples like this where reformers have used alarmist statistics that provided more heat than light.

To understand the role that private money plays in our elections, it's important to understand what I call the "Pyramid of Money." Party leaders such as Republican Tom Delay and Democrat Nancy Pelosi, as well as most incumbents from both parties, don't need to spend a dime on their reelections because they represent one-party fiefdoms due to the red and blue partisan residential patterns and winner-take-all elections. Nevertheless, the big-money kings and queens raise huge amounts of money for their own reelections. Why? Because they use the money for party-building activities and to finance colleagues in the handful of hotly contested races, buying themselves influence among their peers and important party leadership positions. Think of it as a pyramid structure with each party's kings and queens sitting at the top, the fat cats directing the flow of money to the predictably tight races, hoping to win a majority of seats for their team. The rest of the safe-seat incumbents, along with the lobbyists, lawyers, allied PACs, and donors, fill out the lower levels of the Pyramid, funneling money into the Pyramid's labyrinth where it is directed by party leaders who are skilled in the art of deception. It's a well-oiled team operation, with lots of give and take between the different levels of the team.

The Pyramid of Money symbolizes the shape and flow of private money in our political system, and it is fueled by winner-take-all's one-party fiefdoms that allow so many safe-seat incumbents to raise huge amounts of money (which is not needed for their own reelections) so it can be funneled to other partisan activities. The fact that a lot of candidates receive chunks of money from various lobbyists, corporations, and special interests, while definitely a relationship that needs to be monitored and minimized, is not by itself proof that they have been "bought." Oftentimes they are part of the same team because they have the same beliefs and legislative priorities that flow from those beliefs. So when you want to understand the crucial dynamic of money in our politics, don't think of candidates receiving briefcases of money from shadowy lobbyists such as Jack Abramoff. Think of the Pyramid.

Political scientists Jacob Hacker and Paul Pierson describe the modern-day dance between lobbyists and partisan leaders as one where "the stereotyped relationship between the lobbyists and the lobbied" has been turned on its head.[10] Indeed, comments by former House majority leader Tom DeLay reveal the extent to which the lobbyists and special interests today follow the lead of political leaders, not vice versa. Said DeLay, "No one came to me and said, 'Please repeal the Clean Air Act.' We say to the lobbyists, 'Help us.' We know what we want to do and we find the people to help us do that."[11]

Certainly there are notorious examples of riders attached to bills because some quid pro quo occurred between a donor and a powerful political leader. But such riders usually are a small percentage of overall policy and legislation, and most of the time such a blatant quid pro quo affects the donor's personal business situation, not major policy areas—an important distinction. The infamous case of lobbyist Jack Abramoff, who pled guilty to influence peddling and bribery, precisely illustrates the point. Abramoff's activities did not affect major policy areas. Instead, they involved receiving favors from legislators, including from DeLay, for himself and his business clients in exchange for large donations and perks for legislators.[12] DeLay got what he wanted—large donations to grease his political machine— and Abramoff got what he wanted—personal favors for his businesses and clients. They scratched each other's backs, each playing their respective roles in the Pyramid of Money.

So the Pyramid is the problem, much more than the quid pro quo; the quid pro quo is repugnant but only a symptom of the bigger picture. Abramoff and his ilk are hardly the reason DeLay and the GOP pursue right-wing policies. Major policy directions are driven by the dynamics of the Pyramid, with its one-party fiefdoms and kings and queens sitting atop the pile, directing the show.

Certainly it is true that when quid pro quo becomes pervasive, its cumulative effects are corrosive to our democracy because of the public perception of corruption as well as actual corruption of certain policies and appropriations. But it is also true that, even with strong campaign finance reform, breaking up the Pyramid will be very difficult to do as long as we are using a winner-take-all system where most legislative seats are lopsided one-party districts, and invincible incumbents with no worries about reelection can funnel their campaign funds to party leaders sitting atop the Pyramid's labyrinth.

THE PROMISE OF PUBLIC FINANCING

Despite the noxious effects of the Pyramid, public financing of campaigns still can accomplish a lot—though, again, not necessarily for the reasons that many advocates say. The leading brand of public financing today is known as "clean money." Much of the rhetoric from its advocates is aimed at "cleaning up politics," with the implication being that politicians who take private money are "dirty." This ignores the fact that it takes a fair amount of money to communicate with millions of voters; presidential elections obviously are hugely expensive, but so are statewide and congressional races and even many state legislative races. If candidates can't raise enough money to communicate with voters, well-financed, shadowy independent expenditure committees (which are not similarly restricted) will end up becoming *the* dominant source of information for voters. That's a disturbing thought.

Also, the clean money rhetoric undermines our efforts to enact public financing of campaigns because by reinforcing the notion that politicians and money are dirty, crooked, and sleazy, reformers make large segments of the public repulsed at the idea of funding politicians with their taxes and providing "welfare" for the sleazy politicians. It also contributes to a generally negative feeling of the public toward government itself, which feeds into a conservative agenda that for three decades has been bashing government and making the public feel like "government is the problem." If Americans don't value government, then it's not likely they will value democracy, nor will they value reform of that democracy. So the notion of "cleaning up" our politics not only is overhyped; ultimately it is counterproductive and backlashes against our own campaign finance reform efforts.

Here's a more useful—and more accurate—rationale. Public financing allows candidates to chip away at the monolith of the Pyramid of Money by allowing lesser-funded candidates to challenge better-funded candidates and party machines, and to raise issues that foment real campaign debate. It will not unseat the many one-party fiefdoms or destroy the Pyramid—but it can rattle it. Only rarely will it help produce upsets and elect a few more Jesse Venturas (Minnesota's partial public financing and Ventura's inclusion in televised debates certainly were factors in his victory). But given the dynamics of winner-take-all elections combined with partisan residential patterns that create so many safe seats, there's not a lot of wiggle room for upsets to occur. The most effective and accurate rationale in favor of public financing, then, is not one of "cleaning up elections" but one of "opening up the system" and offering "more robust debate" for voters. If public financing is viewed as a matter of *electoral infrastructure*, which, just like election administrators counting votes, is one essential component of holding elections—namely, that of getting political information into the hands of voters—then the logic of public financing becomes crystal clear.

When presented that way, a fair number of incumbents should embrace public campaign financing. It rarely threatens their own reelections, and it frees them from the unpleasant task of "dialing for dollars" in order to fund their campaigns. Most incumbents would enjoy being unshackled from the demands of fund-raising and spending more time with their constituents and actually governing. In fact, more legislative incumbents in Arizona and Maine have begun accepting public financing and opting out of the privately financed system, and why not? It doesn't threaten them politically, and it relieves them of the loathsome pressure of begging for money from well-heeled donors they don't even know.

Given the proper role of public financing in a winner-take-all system—to rattle the Pyramid, to encourage political debate and get information into the hands of voters, and to occasionally contribute to an upset or two—the rules should not be tailored to exclude independents and third party candidates. Alternatives to the major party candidates often are the only hope for shaking things up and reversing the stale formula of the duopoly we now witness as electoral politics. Third parties and independent candidates often have played a role as the "laboratories for new ideas," leading the charge for advancements such as the abolition of slavery, income tax, balanced budgets, women's suffrage, the 40-hour workweek, Social Security, direct election of U.S. senators, and more.[13] Political alternatives should be strongly encouraged, fully funded, and included in televised debates, yet some reformers write their legislation in such a way that only Democratic and Republican candidates have a chance to qualify for public financing.

That's exactly what happened when the Connecticut state legislature passed public financing legislation in December 2005 that blatantly discriminated against independent and third party candidates. Written by a Democratic legislature and a Republican governor with the support of leading campaign finance reform groups, the law forced non–major party candidates into a double eligibility requirement. First they had to gather signatures from 20 percent of voters before they would be allowed to raise qualifying donations necessary to receive public financing; major party candidates, however, were not required to gather any signatures. Lowell Weicker, who was elected governor as a third party candidate of the Connecticut Party in 1990, would have needed 200,000 signatures to become eligible to raise qualifying donations, while the major party candidates he beat would not have had to gather a single signature. This kind of discriminatory approach undermines the good that comes from public financing of campaigns. While it is understandable why leading reformers celebrated another state passing public financing legislation, they did not register even a peep of protest over this discrimination of non–major party candidates. This is cause for concern, since it indicates that reform leaders misunderstand the role that public financing of campaigns plays in our politics.

Public financing measures have succeeded at the ballot box in Maine, Arizona, Massachusetts, Albuquerque, and San Francisco, but losses in Missouri and Oregon have demonstrated that its viability is not a slam dunk. In places where it has been passed, it hasn't produced many electoral upsets or helped "throw the bums out" or clean up politics, as some had unrealistically hoped. But it has minimized money's role and produced more political debate. In Maine, it probably has contributed some to health care reform, not a small achievement. But mostly public financing's success can be measured by the new faces and new voices it has introduced into our politics. That in itself is a significant accomplishment.

FREE MEDIA FOR CANDIDATES

In addition to giving public money to candidates, another promising approach is mandating free radio and television airtime for candidates. Since broadcast media is the greatest expense of any candidate's campaign, especially in the biggest races, this would be a valuable contribution to the quest for robust political debate and challenging the Pyramid. By law, the airwaves are owned by "we the people" but handed over for free to the broadcasting corporations, a nearly $400 billion giveaway. Then those corporations turn around and sell back the airwaves to the candidates, even brazenly jacking up the price of political ads as the election nears. It is such a crooked deal. The government should require broadcasters to provide free airtime to candidates as a condition of receiving their broadcasting license. Mandating free airtime would cost the taxpayer's nothing, but it would significantly reduce the pressure to raise gobs of money in competitive races, as well as enhance political debate.

Free media time for candidates is a practice already used by most established democracies, and it works extremely well. Conservatives and liberals alike are supporting free media time, with Norman Ornstein of the American Enterprise Institute joining with Paul Taylor, formerly of the Alliance for Better Campaigns, to call for the distribution of vouchers for a reasonable amount of free advertising time to candidates and to political parties. They also have called for broadcasters to be required to air a minimum of two hours a week of candidate discussion of issues in the four to six weeks preceding every election. At least half of these segments would have to be aired in prime time or drive time.[14] Senators John McCain (R-AZ), Russell Feingold

(D-WI), and Richard Durbin (D-IL) have introduced the Our Democracy, Our Airwaves Act, which would amend the Communications Act of 1934 to establish minimum airtime requirements on television and radio stations for candidate- and issue-focused programming prior to primary and general elections. The act also would establish a voucher system for the candidates' purchase of commercial broadcast airtime for political advertisements, financed by an annual fee on all broadcast license holders.

While free airtime and public financing will open the political system and foster more debate, it is instructive to note that, as we heard from Judge Abner Mikva and other Illinois legislators, proportional representation also opened the Illinois political system. Not only did it foster more debate, but it actually elected more independent-minded candidates who didn't need as much money to win, even when running against the political machine. That's because proportional voting produces more contested *and* more competitive races. It challenges the Pyramid of Money in a way no other reform can. When combined with public financing and free airtime, it would vastly improve American politics.

Americans should seek to pass public financing and free media time for campaigns at all levels of government—local, state, and federal. Some concerned taxpayers will argue that we can't afford it; I argue we can't afford *not* to have it. We are losing political ideas and stimulating debate at a rapid rate. Publicly financed campaigns and free airtime will help minimize money's role and open up American democracy to new voices and new ideas. Some may see those as only modest improvements compared to the unrealistic goal of "cleaning up politics." But that is the best we can hope for, given the realities of the winner-take-all landscape and the limits imposed by a dreadful Supreme Court decision that equates money with speech. Still, public financing of campaigns and free media time hold considerable promise for improving our democracy, and we should work vigorously for their enactment.

▣ Summary of Reforms

1. Support public financing of all campaigns at local, state, and federal levels.
2. Demand free media time for candidates on radio and TV— support McCain, Feingold, and Durbin's Our Democracy, Our Airwaves Act.
3. Include third party and independent candidates in public financing and televised debates.
4. Set appropriate donation limits.
5. Set appropriate spending caps on candidates (if we can sneak it by the Supreme Court).

▣ Organizations to Contact

Public Campaign, **www.publicampaign.org**, (202) 293-0222

Common Cause, **www.commoncause.org**, (202) 833-1200

The Campaign Legal Center, **www.campaignlegalcenter.org**, (202) 736-2200

League of Women Voters, **www.lwv.org**, (202) 429-1965

Free Air Time Campaign, **www.freeairtime.org**, 1-888-6FreeTV

U.S. PIRG, **www.uspirg.org**, (202) 546-9707

TheRestofUs.org, (916) 446-4741

9

Reform the Supreme Court

The 2000 presidential election was a difficult moment in our nation's history. Recall the partisan clashes and low-intensity violence that occurred on the picket lines outside the hand counts in Florida. Protesters in combat fatigues and blackface eerily stood out, holding aloft signs saying things such as "Bush or Revolution," with *Revolution* written in bloody scrawl. Other placards read, "God Made Bush President." Threatening letters were mailed to judges, including one with an illustration of a skull and crossbones.[1] Political leaders on both sides were no less riled. Certain southern GOP legislators, sounding like the ghosts of John C. Calhoun and Jefferson Davis, spouted incendiary threats about state's rights and defying the Florida courts, and Tom DeLay called the election "a theft in progress."[2] The Gore camp moved aggressively for a recount of only a handful of heavily Democratic counties rather than the entire state, where numerous irregularities also had occurred, perpetuating partisanship and dooming the principle of "count every vote."

Into this harrowing breach stepped the United States Supreme Court. As adjudicators of the supreme law of the land, this was their moment to shine like a brilliant beacon and show the world how democracy is practiced. Glued to our television sets, radios, and websites, we held our collective breath, waiting for what we assumed to be the top legal minds of our nation to sort this out. But we all know what happened next. The Supreme Court revealed itself to be just another partisan legislature—and an unelected one at that. Any illusion that the Supreme Court is an impartial body was detonated by its 5–4 decision that made George W. Bush president.

Between the November 7 election and the Court's December 12 decision, conflicts of interest and signs of partisan motives emerged among several of the justices. *Newsweek* and the *Wall Street Journal* reported a disquieting episode in which Justice Sandra Day O'Connor, attending an election night party surrounded by friends and acquaintances, exclaimed, "This is terrible," when CBS called Florida for Al Gore. A visibly shaken O'Connor explained disgustedly to another partygoer that the election was "over." O'Connor's husband clarified her uncharacteristic outburst by saying his wife was upset because they had wanted to retire, and O'Connor, a Reagan appointee, didn't want a Democrat to name her successor.[3] Conflicts of interest appeared in regard to Justices Scalia and Thomas as well. Scalia's son was a partner in the law firm representing Bush and his legal challenge before the U.S. Supreme Court, and Thomas's wife was working at the conservative Heritage Foundation as a headhunter, gathering résumés for appointments in the soon-to-be Bush administration.

Even so, legal experts were unprepared for a decision of such magnitude to be so blatantly partisan. The flimsy legal justification cited by the Rehnquist-Scalia majority set off a firestorm, with criticism from conservative and liberal experts alike exploding in the media and on op-ed pages. Yale law professor Akhil Reed Amar noted that the majority "failed to cite a single case that, on its facts, comes close to supporting its analysis and result."[4] Terrance Sandalow, the conservative dean of the University of Michigan law school who opposed *Roe v. Wade* and supported the nomination of Robert Bork to the Court, called the stay of the Florida recount "an unmistakably partisan decision without any foundation in law."[5] Michael Greve of the American Enterprise Institute wrote in the conservative *The Weekly Standard*, "It would be silly to deny that partisan considerations influenced . . . the justices' rulings."[6] Even Bush's own lawyer in the Florida lawsuits, Ted Olson, was surprised when the High Court issued an unusual emergency order on December 9 to stop the hand recount of ballots in Florida.[7] One prominent attorney thought that the most unusual aspect of the outpouring of sharp criticism was "how few conservative voices you hear out there defending the decision. . . . The silence on the conservative side is more telling than the yelling on the left."[8]

Hand recounts to settle close elections are fairly common, the most recent high-profile example being the statewide recount of the 2004 Washington governor's race, which was decided by 129 votes and had to be hand recounted three times. But in *Bush v. Gore*, the Supreme Court majority voted inexplicably to end the hand recounts in Florida. And they provided a preposterously thin legal precedent for the ruling—the Fourteenth Amendment's Equal Protection Clause, which has been used historically to remedy racial discrimination.

The High Court ruled, not unreasonably, that those voters living in counties using a stricter standard for hand recounts had an "unequal" chance of having their votes count. But the Supremes missed the glaringly obvious contradiction that the same logic should have been applied to the antiquated, error-prone Votomatic punch card machines themselves. Voters living in Votomatic precincts and counties, where numerous punch card votes had been lost, had an "unequal" chance of having *their* votes counted, too, compared with voters in counties using optical scan or touch screen machines. Ironically, given the Court's invocation of a Fourteenth Amendment "equality" claim, those equipment malfunctions disproportionately hurt minority voters, and a hand recount was the only way to overcome this well-known defect of the Votomatics. So if the overriding legal objection was lack of a statewide standard for recounts, the High Court could have resolved this easily by ordering the Florida

Supreme Court to fashion a single statewide standard and continuing the recount with that standard.

Instead, the Supreme Court halted the Florida recount entirely. In essence, the Supreme Court ruled, in a bitterly divided 5–4 decision, that it was perfectly fine that affluent and mostly white voters in precincts using modern voting equipment enjoyed a better chance of having their votes counted than minority, poor, and elderly voters in precincts using antiquated punch card machines. But when it came time to hand-recount ballots to overcome this preelection advantage, the Supreme Court slammed shut the constitutional gates. Bewilderingly, even after George W. Bush was declared the 43rd president, thousands of Florida ballots still sat in piles across the state, having never been counted because the antiquated punch card machines could not tally them, and a hand recount like that used in many other states for close elections was aborted.

Almost as a way of covering their clumsy tracks, the Rehnquist-Scalia majority took the highly unusual step of issuing their decision as an unsigned and anonymous *per curiam* opinion, which usually is reserved for unanimous opinions in unimportant cases.[9] The four justices in the minority issued four stinging dissents, but even more disturbing was that the majority inserted what the *New York Times* called an "odd disclaimer" near the end of its decision: "Our consideration is limited to the present circumstances, for the problem of equal protection in election processes generally presents many complexities."[10] In other words, this ruling was not to apply in any other case. It was a one-shot deal and not to be used as a precedent for any future Fourteenth Amendment/Equal Protection challenges to unfair election procedures or to antiquated voting machines of the type that disproportionately hurt black, poor, and elderly voters in Florida. It was as if the Court majority had changed the rules of the game in order to win and now, having won, had changed the rules back again.

All legal scholars could do was shake their heads and mutter a by-then well-known Rehnquist-Scalia court truism: "Five votes beats a reason any day." Which is the same thing you would expect to say about a legislature, where it's not uncommon for raw naked partisanship to prevail over comity and scholarly discourse. Indeed, the Republican majority on the Supreme Court voted in the winner as if it *were* a legislature. *Bush v. Gore* has contributed to a loss of legitimacy usually reserved for politicians: A recent opinion poll found that only 40 percent of Americans now hold a favorable view of the Supreme Court.[11]

SUPREME COURT REFORM

The obvious partisanship of their decision casts the Supreme Court in a whole new light. If it's going to act like a legislature, then should its members remain unelected? Or if appointment is still the preferred selection process for a justice, should it be for a life term? And should the president remain the sole appointing authority, and the highly unrepresentative Senate the sole confirming authority? Previously few experts would have questioned the constitutional structure of the third branch of government, but *Bush v. Gore* has changed that.

The partisan tension has played out most dramatically over lifelong appointments to the Court. This was highlighted during the nomination in 2005 of Chief Justice John Roberts who, at 50 years of age at the time of his nomination, easily could serve for three decades. More than any other single factor, this "until death do we part" constitutional requirement has been responsible for bruising and bitter confirmation battles. On the partisan chessboard, nailing down a lifetime Supreme Court spot is a major victory for your side.

In fact, justices are serving longer and longer terms. Between 1941 and 1970, the average justice's tenure was 12.2 years. Since then, the average term has been 25.6 years. The average age of a justice leaving office has risen from 67.6 years to a very elderly 78.8 years. At the time of Roberts's nomination, two justices had been on the Supreme Court for more than 30 years.[12] Appointees to the Court used to be much older, with typical appointees being distinguished elders whose appointment was considered a capstone to a career in law or public service. Now presidents look for some young buck with no paper trail whom they can install for decades. As a result, the appointment process has become an obtuse guessing game, with opponents searching high and low for some long-lost letter, speech, or paper that gives a clue as to the nominee's true mind-set. They parry back and forth across the divide of the Senate Judiciary Committee, with the nominee saying as little as possible, an unsatisfying defensive dodge. The nation watches bewildered and wonders, How can a person with no apparent opinions be fit for the highest court in the land?

Lifetime court appointments are the root cause of this increasingly perplexing ritual, and it's time to get rid of them. Most other democracies, as well as nearly all our states, employ judicial term limits, usually with no chance of reappointment. High Court justices in Germany are limited to a 12-year term; and in France, Italy, and Spain, a 9-year term. Of all our state courts, only the Rhode Island state supreme court has life tenure.[13] Judges on the U.S. Court of Federal Claims are limited to 15-year terms.[14] Norman Ornstein, a scholar with the conservative American Enterprise Institute, has written in favor of 15-year term limits for Supreme Court justices and federal appeals court judges.[15] Many liberal experts agree.

Ironically, Chief Justice Roberts himself supported judicial term limits earlier in his career. In a 1983 memo, Roberts, who was working in the Reagan White House, noted that the Framers "adopted life tenure at a time when people simply did not live as long as they do now." He reasoned that long-entrenched judges could fall out of step with the society they serve. "A judge insulated from the normal currents of life for 25 or 30 years was a rarity then but is becoming commonplace today. Setting a term of, say, 15 years would ensure that federal judges would not lose all touch with reality through decades of ivory tower existence."[16] Twenty years later, facing a lifetime appointment as chief justice, Roberts had little to say on the subject.

Defenders of the status quo view any tampering of the Supreme Court appointment process as an assault on judicial independence. They argue that the Founding Fathers wanted to insulate the Court from partisan politics and believed life tenure was the solution. But, as Bruce Bartlett with the National Center for Policy Analysis has written, the Founding Fathers also saw no need to limit presidential terms, yet that didn't stop us from amending the Constitution to do so. Ornstein has written, "A 15-year term [without the possibility of reappointment] would still provide insulation from political pressure; that tenure is seven years longer than any president can serve." Members of the Federal Reserve Board, who it is believed also ought to be shielded from politics because they oversee the nation's economy, serve 14-year terms.

According to a 2004 poll, 60 percent of Americans say it is time to limit Court terms.[17] The bitter partisanship of the current process has deeply undercut all notions of justice and fairness. If justices are prohibited from reappointment, there is no reason to believe limiting them to 15 or 18 years—longer than most justices have served, historically—wouldn't also achieve judicial independence without the bitter partisanship connected to the current appointment process. Staggered terms of 15 to 18 years would create an opening about every 2 years so each president serving a full term likely would make two appointments, providing more of a long-term ideological balance to the Court.

Besides judicial term limits, some nations require that High Court justices retire at a certain age. In Canada, the retirement age is 75; in Israel and Australia, age 70. Some American states also have established a retirement age for judges, 70 years in the case of Minnesota and Missouri. If applied to the current Supreme Court at the time of the Roberts's nomination, three justices already would have retired, with two more stepping down in 2006. Increasingly, a mandatory retirement age of 70 to 75 years and a judicial term limit of 15 to 18 years make sense for ensuring the esteem and legitimacy of the third branch into the 21st century.

Who Should Appoint and Confirm the Supreme Court?

Currently the president appoints and the Senate confirms Supreme Court nominees. It is worth considering multiple appointing authorities for the justices as a way of balancing the ideological slant of the Court over time. In France, Germany, Italy, South Africa, and Spain, no single person, office, or institution has a monopoly on appointments to the constitutional court. Typically, this authority is shared between the upper and lower houses of the parliament, and the president or prime minister. In Spain, four judges are appointed by the upper house, four by the lower house, two by the government, and two by a Judges Council. In France, nominations for judges to its High Council come not only from the government but also from other judges and a public prosecutor.[18]

Bipartisan appointments also hold promise for ensuring the court's ideological breadth. One way of creating bipartisan appointments is to require a confirmation vote of 60 senators out of 100 instead of a simple majority. Since no one party usually would have 60 votes, that would nudge the parties toward bipartisan consensus. Doug Cassel, director of the Center for International Human Rights of the Northwestern University School of Law, notes that most European countries require a three-fifths or two-thirds majority to select judges of their highest courts. In Germany, each of the two houses of parliament elects half the 16 constitutional court judges with a two-thirds majority. Since neither party can achieve two-thirds on its own, the predictable result is that parties usually acquiesce to each other's nominees, producing judges representing a balance of the two major parties and achieving a bit of proportional representation on Germany's High Court.[19]

Requiring 60 votes also would be an acknowledgment of how distorted representation in the U.S. Senate is. Recall that of 100 senators, only 14 are women and 6 are racial minorities. Also recall that the Senate gives low-population states such as Wyoming far more representation per capita than high-population states such as California. The net effect is to give a representation subsidy to conservative red states, resulting in Republicans enjoying a lopsided 55–44 Senate majority even though they won fewer Senate votes than Democrats. That "representation quota" has overrepresented the Republican Party in every election since 1958.[20] A strong case can be made that a chamber as unrepresentative as the United States Senate should not be confirming lifetime appointments—especially not by simple majority vote. Doing so ensures that the unrepresentative nature of the Senate is spread to the third branch of government.

The subject of proportional representation on the Supreme Court—which is the notion that the justices should, to some reasonable degree, reflect the partisan and ideological makeup of the country—is a subject that has not been considered enough. But in the *Bush v. Gore* era, where it has become glaringly apparent that the Supreme Court is, after all, a political and even a partisan body—just like a legislature—its unrepresentative nature becomes all the more objectionable. Of the current nine justices, it is likely that at least six are Republicans, two are Democrats, with perhaps one independent or another Republican seated, in a nation where partisan sympathies are divided evenly. Of the 13 justices who served during the 20 years of the Rehnquist Court, 10 were appointed by Republican presidents and only 3 by a Democratic president. Supreme Court expert Mark

Tushnet writes, "The story of the Rehnquist Court is the story of a Court divided . . . between two types of Republicans," while the Court's badly outnumbered liberals "mostly sat on the sidelines."[21]

But then the terms *liberal* and *moderate* always have been used loosely by the media in analyzing the Supreme Court. In the narrowly construed ideological spectrum applied to the Court, John Paul Stevens—who was appointed by a Republican president and voted to reinstate capital punishment and oppose affirmative action—is a liberal. So is David Souter, also appointed by a Republican president, who voted to uphold parade organizers' refusal to allow a gay Irish group to march in the St. Patrick's Day parade and to allow federal authorities to prosecute sick people who smoke marijuana on doctors' orders. Sandra Day O'Connor, a former Republican majority leader of the Arizona state senate and Reagan appointee who voted with ultraconservative Rehnquist 71 percent of the time and Stevens only 33 percent, is known as a judicial moderate.[22] Ruth Bader Ginsburg is considered an ultraliberal, despite her centrist voting record when she sat on a closely divided appeals court and sided more often with Republican-appointed judges (including then-judges Kenneth Starr and Robert Bork) than with those judges chosen by Democrats.[23] When Democrats are pining for the recently retired O'Connor, it's clear the Court has lost its ideological balance.

A Supreme Court liberal is nothing like a Ted Kennedy or Jesse Jackson liberal. Many a "liberal" on the Supreme Court would have been considered a centrist in any other legislative body, and the moderates such as O'Connor and Anthony Kennedy would be considered conservatives. But our perceptions about judicial political orientation have become grossly distorted because we have come to expect that the Senate-confirmed justices naturally will incorporate the Senate's unrepresentative bias. The fact is, the current Supreme Court is an extremely conservative body badly out of step with the values and beliefs of mainstream America. What this view reinforces is that the Senate should not be the only filter between the president and lifetime appointments to the Supreme Court.

THE IMMODERATE COURT

Analyzing the Supreme Court as an ideologically skewed "judicial legislature" is not simply an academic exercise in partisan bean counting. There's plenty of evidence that it matters. Beyond the indefensible *Bush v. Gore*, other Supreme Court decisions in recent years have dramatically rolled back the rights of all Americans. Whether ruling on issues related to civil liberties, telecommunications, voting rights for minorities, campaign finance reform, media consolidation, or even leafleting in shopping malls, the Rehnquist-Scalia court consistently was on the side of the plutocrats, corporations, and special interests.

Some of their radical decisions have held that citizens have no constitutionally protected right to an education (much less an equal one); that weirdly shaped congressional districts are permissible for incumbent and party protection, but not for electing racial minorities; that publicly funded television channels can sponsor closed debates between Democrats and Republicans that exclude independent or third party candidates; and that private corporations have a constitutional right to spend unlimited amounts of cash to influence public initiative and referendum campaigns. The Scalia-Rehnquist Five also struck down, stripped down, or gutted the Religious Freedom Restoration Act, the Gun-Free School Zones Act, the Brady Handgun Violence Prevention Act, the Violence against Women Act, parts of the Age Discrimination in Employment Act, the Low-Level Radioactive Waste Policy Act, parts of the Fair Labor Standards Act, and certain applications of the Americans with Disability Act, often on states' rights grounds—one of the battle cries of the old

Confederacy.[24] The Supreme Court's 2001–2002 term was a particularly troubling one. In cases concerning school vouchers and church-state separation, the rights of Americans with disabilities, federalism versus states' rights, and the privacy rights of students, the Court significantly restricted civil and constitutional rights and federal authority.[25]

The "judicial legislature" of the Supreme Court decided a number of these cases by narrow 5–4 votes in which ultra-conservative Justices Scalia, Thomas, and Rehnquist played a critical role in helping push the Court in a rightward direction. Even as the Court's majority claimed to be merely interpreting the law, numerous legal experts argued that the five-justice conservative majority engineered some of the most extreme judicial activism. Friendships between justices and leading right-wingers such as Scalia and Vice President Dick Cheney, who go duck hunting together, have added more suspicion to the sense that the Court's decisions are driven by partisanship, not jurisprudence—just like a legislature, not a court of law.

Judicial term limits, mandatory retirement ages, higher confirmation thresholds, and multiple appointing authorities would bring some partisan balance to this "judicial legislature." Proportionate partisanship in the courts would help seat not only brilliant legal minds but a balance of legal perspectives and help prevent a partisan monoculture from dominating our judicial system. In these times of extreme partisan polarization, that would be good for America.

CURTAILING THE HIDDEN POWERS
OF THE CHIEF JUSTICE

The position of chief justice today wields tremendous power behind the scenes, much more than was intended originally by the Constitution, and the public is little aware of it. Law professors

Judith Resnik and Theodore Ruger, in an important article written for the *New York Times*, gave a thumbnail sketch of these acquired powers that should cause great concern.

Besides being highly visible and influential as the presiding officer at the Court's public sessions and in selecting each Court opinion's author, the chief justice also has tremendous authority over the vast federal judicial bureaucracy, as well as influence in Congress. The chief justice is the chief executive officer of a giant, sprawling federal bureaucracy of some 1,200 life-tenured judges, 850 magistrate and bankruptcy judges, and a staff of 30,000, including overseeing its budget, now about $5.4 billion annually—not that much less than the budget for the entire Environmental Protection Agency.[26] But the situation gets more interesting.

The chief justice is the chair of the policy-setting body known as the Judicial Conference of the United States that establishes the priorities for the federal judiciary, and he (so far all chief justices have been men) appoints the director of the Administrative Office of the United States Courts. Together they select the judges who sit on judicial committees focused on topics ranging from technology to international judicial relations, policy recommendations with respect to legal reform, reform of court procedures, and advocating for the federal courts. Resnik and Ruger write that with Chief Justice Rehnquist acting as the "lobbyist in chief," these judicial committees became activist oriented, lobbying Congress to enact their agenda. This agenda included opposition to creating any new federal rights to be enforced through the federal courts, but the "lobbyist in chief" and his cohorts didn't stop there. The Judicial Conference overseen by Rehnquist also took positions on various bills pending in Congress. In the early 1990s, it opposed creating a new civil rights action for victims of gender-motivated violence proposed as part of legislation on violence against women. It subsequently retreated from this position, but in 2000, six years after Congress had enacted the Violence against Women Act, Chief Justice

Rehnquist wrote the majority opinion overturning that law, ruling 5 to 4 that Congress had trampled on states' rights in bestowing that new civil right.

The chief justice also selects judges to serve on the Alien Terrorist Removal Court, which decides deportation cases of legal aliens suspected of aiding terrorism. He also holds great power over government surveillance by selecting the 11 judges who sit for seven-year terms on the Foreign Intelligence Surveillance Act Court. Since its creation in 1978, this court has approved over 10,000 government requests for surveillance warrants.[27] This little-known court briefly was in the public spotlight when it was leaked in late 2005 that the Bush administration had been conducting wiretaps and surveillance on Americans without seeking this court's approval, as Bush was legally bound to do.

Yes, the chief justice of the United States is a busy little beaver, behind closed doors. According to Resnick and Ruger, "The administrative role of the chief justice is a 20th-century invention, not a constitutional mandate. That role, and the additional stature that comes to the chief, are the product of some 100 ad hoc Congressional statutes and the ambitions of those who held the office." Chief Justice Rehnquist went further than any previous chief justice, "skillfully using the interaction of his administrative and adjudicative roles to shape the law of the land."

So Chief Justice Roberts, who easily could serve in that capacity for 30 years, now oversees these sorts of activities, most of them shielded from public scrutiny. Yet during his confirmation hearings in September 2005, he was asked only two brief and perfunctory questions about the chief justice's pivotal role.[28] It was barely a blip on the Senate Judiciary Committee's radar screen, despite how much power is invested in the chief justice's job description.

So what can be done about this arrangement? Resnick and Ruger point out that a judicial position that wields so much unchecked power for so long is anomalous—and potentially dangerous. Accordingly, the following recommendations make sense. First, it's necessary to disperse the chief justice's power by separating the jobs of administration from adjudication, to insulate them from each other. It's not uncommon for judges to share power with other judges, such as judges on appellate courts who engage in a collective enterprise, and trial judges who are subject to appellate review. Second, the chief justice and other parts of the federal judiciary over which he presides should be prohibited from lobbying elected leaders unless it is for a legislative bill that directly affects the operations of the judicial bureaucracy. Especially lobbying for or against any issue-related legislation should be strictly prohibited. Third, openness and sunshine. Too much of the chief justice's administrative activity is conducted behind closed doors, without public scrutiny. Administrative decisions should be subject to oversight and disclosure, just as Supreme Court decisions are.

If the Supreme Court is going to act and vote like a judicial legislature, then it should be treated accordingly. In this era of the 49–49 nation, where even the third branch of government—the judicial conscience charged with refereeing the other two branches and upholding the nation's constitutional principles—has been infected by the stain of partisanship, it is time to remake this antiquated 18th-century institution. Without substantive reform, the Supreme Court will continue to lose legitimacy in the eyes of the public. The stigma of *Bush v. Gore* still haunts us in the eye rolling that now accompanies each Supreme Court decision, as observers shake their heads and pronounce what everyone knows to be true: "Five votes beats a reason, any day."

■ Summary of Recommendations

1. Set judicial term limits of 15- to 18-year terms, with no reappointment.
2. Establish a mandatory retirement age of 70 to 75 years old.

3. Set higher confirmation thresholds, 60 percent or two-thirds.
4. Designate multiple appointing authorities.
5. Remove confirmation powers from the unrepresentative Senate and give them to the House.

For the Chief Justice

1. Disperse the power; separate the jobs of administration from adjudication.
2. Prohibit lobbying elected leaders about any pending legislation unless it is related to the operations of the federal judicial bureaucracy.
3. Encourage openness and sunshine—lift the veil of secrecy shrouding the chief justice's administrative power.

10

Restore Faith in Government: "Government Is Good for You"

Hurricane Katrina blew in from the Gulf of Mexico with a destructive force that was nearly beyond comprehension. It was of September 11–like proportions, apocalyptic in its impact, except this time there was no culprit to blame for the destruction.

Yet fingers pointed in all directions following the government's feeble relief response. The governor of Louisiana accused the feds, the feds accused the states, President Bush accused Mother Nature, and the mayor of New Orleans accused everyone. With the poorest and most vulnerable Americans taking the brunt of it, the rest of the nation watched the rising pools of water drown an entire region, its people, and one of America's great iconic cities. We had front row seats to a colossal governmental failure the likes of which had not been seen in decades. For many, the government's response raised uncomfortable questions about racism and poverty in America, as well as homeland security.

The episode also made some Americans more pessimistic about our government's ability to do anything right. But many other Americans reached a different conclusion. If the government and its various agencies had been better prepared for this entirely predictable natural catastrophe, the damage and death toll would have been much reduced. The better conclusion, they believed, was that effective government can improve our lives, both in times of crisis and over the long haul. Yvonne Lee, former commissioner with the U.S. Commission on Civil Rights, wrote an op-ed in the midst of the Hurricane Katrina fallout. "Unfortunately," she wrote, "the far right have for years asserted that the federal government is a problem, not a solution in Americans' lives. Yet Katrina has served as a costly reminder that the federal government can, and must, serve the public good."[1]

In this sense, Katrina dramatized a long-standing debate in American politics and society. Going back to before Ronald Reagan's presidency, the right wing had mounted an ideological campaign to malign government and portray it as an impediment to a better society. Reagan declared boldly in his first inaugural address, "Government is not the solution to our problem; government *is* the problem."[2] Newt Gingrich continued this ideological attack by portraying government as an ineffectual bumbler and sugar daddy for welfare queens. George W. Bush poured it on in his bid to enact huge tax cuts that mostly benefited the wealthy. Grover Norquist, a leading conservative, famously stated, "I don't want to abolish government; I simply want to reduce it to the size where I can drag it into the bathroom and drown it in the bathtub."[3] Bill Clinton signed up the Democrats for this detail when, with one eye on reelection, he declared in his 1995 State of the Union address that the "era of big government is over." Like the Republicans, Clinton used the scapegoating of welfare mothers and the poor as a political stepping-stone.

So for some time now, political opportunists of all stripes have been scapegoating government to win elections, even if it means undermining government itself. Indeed, one has to go back as far as President John F. Kennedy to find an American leader capable of eloquently combining the right mix of idealism and pragmatism about the role of government. In a 1962 commencement speech, JFK portrayed government as having great potential to be a positive force: "There are three great areas of our domestic affairs in which, today, there is a danger that illusion may prevent effective action," he said. "They are, first, the question of the size and the shape of government's responsibilities; secondly, the question of public fiscal policy; and third, the matter of . . . confidence in America." President Kennedy then outlined his view about the proper role of government. He framed the discourse by asking two key questions: "How do we eradicate the barriers which separate substantial minorities of our citizens from access to education and employment on equal terms with the rest?" And "How, in sum, can we make our free economy work at full capacity—that is, provide adequate profits for enterprise, adequate wages for labor, and opportunity for all?"

In recent years, America's political leaders have answered those questions by blaming government and denigrating its role. At the same time, they have promoted the individual as the essential actor, culminating in George W. Bush's atomistic conception of an "ownership society." Yet the faces of the poor blacks in New Orleans, flailing on TV against the floodwaters, unable to escape like the better-off whites and blacks, strike at the heart of the prevailing ideology that "government is the problem." Who will deny that, for hundreds of thousands from New Orleans and the Gulf Coast, whether Republican, Democrat, or independent, they wished they had had more government, not less, prior to the storm and in the days afterward? Government clearly has a role to play in bettering our lives, yet like their political leaders, many Americans have gotten used to diminished expectations. After decades of conservative attacks, the government's reputation has been damaged, and the public's confidence in government has waned. To some degree, a self-fulfilling prophecy is at work here, for if we don't expect government to work, it probably won't.

As public confidence in government declines, the widespread appreciation for representative democracy itself is atrophying, like shriveled grapes on a vine. If the American people don't have much use for government, then what use is democracy?

What does it matter if voting equipment failure or poor ballot design causes the wrong candidate to win the presidency? And what does it matter if minority voters are facing increasing levels of harassment and disenfranchisement? Or what does it matter if there is so little competition in congressional races, or voter turnout has declined to single digits in many races, or our legislatures are polarizing with fewer moderate bridge builders getting elected? If you don't value government, you probably won't value the means by which we elect the government and so breakdowns in the democratic process are greeted with a collective shrug. Thus, this ideological attack on government has formed the philosophical underpinnings for an attack on representative democracy itself.

The reputation of government in the United States is suffering from a massive public relations crisis. It gets no credit for the good things it does, and all the blame and scorn for its mistakes. That attitude is hurting our country. If we want to understand not only the feebleness of the government's response to a natural disaster, but also how so many poor and minority Americans could be so vulnerable to begin with, we have to come to grips with how this all-too-American attitude that "government is the problem" and "government is bad for you" has led us to this point.

"GOVERNMENT IS GOOD FOR YOU"

Most of the Founders and Framers begrudgingly accepted government as a necessary evil. James Madison, in a backhanded defense of government, stated, "It has been said that all Government is evil. It would be more proper to say that the necessity of any government is a misfortune. This necessity however exists; and the problem to be solved is, not what form of government is perfect, but which of the forms is least imperfect."[4] This ambivalence explains why Madison and his contemporaries loaded so many antidemocratic tendencies into our Constitution, especially the structures of the Senate and the Electoral College. They were suspicious of "we the people."

But by the 1830s, Americans were no longer so skeptical of government. With a little democratic experience under their belts and the benefits of a growing and prospering nation, Americans viewed their government more as a useful democratic instrument. Commenting on our 19th-century predecessors, Alexis de Tocqueville observed in 1832, "Everyone takes as zealous an interest in the affairs of the township, his county, and the whole State, as if they were his own. The citizen looks upon the fortune of the public as his own, and he labors for the good of the State."[5]

More recently, Americans can point to many public sector achievements. Whether the service is mail delivery, the care of seniors via Social Security and Medicare, the construction of roads and highways, telecommunications, hospitals, schools, defense, scientific research, national parks, railroads, airways and waterways, environmental protection, the Internet, and much, much more, government has been the leading player, oftentimes partnering with America's businesses, other times restraining business from doing harm to workers, communities, and the environment. Government has been the driving force behind regulating the economy, interest rates, and inflation as well as creating policies that grow and maintain the middle class, such as pro–home ownership, worker protections, the 40-hour workweek, and paid vacations and holidays. And, yes, the federal government has been there many times in the past to shoulder the burden following natural disasters. The United States is acknowledged by all four corners as the world's leading superpower, the wealthiest and most powerful nation in human history—how could we have achieved that status if government was such a bumbler? Americans' myopia on this point is astounding.

This is not to excuse the mistakes that government makes, which at times have been considerable. But the same conservatives who portray government as evil usually portray the private sector as a shining example of competence and virtue. In fact, recent financial meltdowns in the corporate world, the gouging of American ratepayers by energy and oil companies, and the fleecing of taxpayers by Halliburton are just the latest examples of a long record of crooked and inept businesses. Perhaps the greatest corporate scandal in the history of the United States was the savings and loan collapse in the late 1980s, which occurred as a result of the Reagan administration's deregulation policies. Approximately 1,000 S&Ls had to be closed, costing taxpayers an extraordinary $153 billion, easily the most expensive financial sector crisis the world has ever seen. Grandmas and grandpas lost their life savings, showing what can happen when government gets out of the way and leaves business to itself. Recent corporate bankruptcies and financial scandals from Enron, WorldCom, Qwest, and others have cost taxpayers billions more and stranded their employees with vanished pension plans.[6] Incredibly, Enron was one of the most celebrated businesses of the 1990s, with *Fortune* magazine naming it "America's Most Innovative Company" for six consecutive years, showing the poor judgment of those excoriating government as "the problem."[7]

But under the withering attacks from conservatives, government has been held to a different standard than business. This duplicity must be confronted if American government—and, by extension, representative democracy—are ever to receive their due. While Americans display a high degree of patriotism, most of that is not identified with "the government" but with "the nation." This bifurcation in the American mind-set is a distortion of reality and substantially a result of the relentless right-wing antigovernment propaganda blitz. Instead of conducting a constructive conversation about the proper role of government and its achievements versus its mistakes, we have made government bashing an electoral sport. In the 49–49 nation, the discourse about government has become entangled in the partisan war, with both Democrats and Republicans scoring points using government as a scapegoat.

But President Kennedy tried to move this discussion away from partisanship. He said, way back in 1962:

> What is at stake in our economic decisions today is not some grand warfare of rival ideologies which will sweep the country with passion, but the practical management of a modern economy. What we need is not labels and clichés but more basic discussion of the sophisticated and technical questions involved in keeping a great economic machinery moving ahead.

Kennedy's vision of government's role in the "practical management of a modern economy" and in "keeping a great economic machinery moving ahead" has been lost over the decades. Instead, both major political parties leapfrog each other to win votes from fiscally conservative swing voters who want smaller government, tax cuts, and less money for government programs. As a result, America has lost much of its sense of social solidarity, becoming the ultimate "free lunch society" where no one's government program is more deserving than your own. Middle-class and upper-middle-class home owners, working hard at their 9-to-5 jobs, sometimes look cynically at government programs that would have helped the needy and vulnerable of New Orleans. But they are more than willing to pocket their Bush tax cuts and home mortgage deductions, which can easily amount to many thousands of dollars per year. If they own a small business, they also can pocket an outrageous tax deduction when they buy an SUV, amounting to $60,000 on a $100,000 vehicle.[8] Hummers getting 10 miles per gallon cost not much more than a Toyota Prius hybrid, even as American soldiers die in the Middle East trying to secure the oil supply. Many of the poor in urban areas don't even own a car, so federal and state subsidies for roads don't benefit them as they benefit middle-class commuters. Likewise, subsidies for sports stadiums, symphonies, ballets, operas, and other amenities often benefit the well-off but not many poorer Americans.

America will not regain that Kennedyesque vision until government is rehabilitated in the eyes of Americans. Reagan declared that "government is the problem," but Kennedy offered a different path, one that acknowledges that government also has been good for America. It includes an admission that, sure, government makes mistakes, but so does big business, and government often has been part of the solution. It's not so black-and-white, and as more and more Americans realize this point, the era of Reagan's "cut to the bone" government will end. Big government, having been eclipsed by limited government, will be replaced by "smart government."

RESTORING FAITH IN "SMART GOVERNMENT"

Smart government is different from the much-maligned "big government." Smart government uses its unique capacity to bring people together and to pass laws and regulate businesses and services in such a way that the effort actually helps businesses and the people who work for them. In return, business is expected to contribute its fair share and to take responsibility for its crucial role as an employer.

For instance, Montana governor Brian Schweitzer needed to figure out how to get quality affordable health care to many Montanans working for smaller businesses. Small businesses are the engine of Montana's economy, yet oftentimes it's difficult for small businesses to afford skyrocketing health care premiums for their employees. Governor Schweitzer called for and signed into law a program creating a purchasing pool allowing small businesses to band together to negotiate and purchase affordable health insurance for their employees. Participating employers and employees who join the health insurance pool receive assistance payments for a portion of their health insurance premiums, funded by tobacco tax revenues.

This program is a good example of smart government. Government smartly used its unique capacity to bring people together and to pass laws and regulations in a way that not only helped people get health care but also helped small businesses solve a real problem. Across the nation, soaring health care costs are one of the most perplexing dilemmas of the business climate today, and smart government should be able to help solve the problem.

Another example of smart government applied to health care has been happening in the most unlikely of places: veterans hospitals. Ten years ago, these hospitals were dangerous, dirty, scandal ridden, and giving government a bad name. Today, they're producing the highest-quality care in the country, according to several studies, including one from the National Committee for Quality Assurance.[9] The turnaround began in 1994 under a new chief, Kenneth Kizer, who systematically improved quality and the level of safety that to this day are largely lacking in the corporatized private health care system. How did the Veterans Hospital Administration (VHA) do this? The answer is involved, but one crucial component has been called "laptop medicine." The VHA developed state-of-the-art software that allows for the best tracking and medical diagnosis in the entire health care industry. The software plays a key role in preventing medical errors and medication mistakes, which a scandalous 1999 report from the Institute of Medicine showed has been the cause of death in the privatized health care system for an astounding 98,000 hospital patients per year, as many as 4 percent of all annual deaths in the United States.

Today VHA doctors enter their orders and prescriptions into their laptops which immediately check them against the patient's records. If the various doctors working with a patient have prescribed an inappropriate combination of medicines, the computer sends up a red flag. When hospital pharmacists fill the prescription, the computer system generates a bar code that goes on the bottle and registers what the medicine is, who it is for, when it should be administered, and in what dose. Each patient also has an ID bracelet with its own bar code, and so does each nurse. Before administering any drug, a nurse must first scan the patient's ID bracelet, then her own, and then the bar code on the medicine. If she has the wrong patient or medicine, the computer will alert her. The computer will also create a report if the nurse is late in administering a dose. Electronic records were crucial in helping VHA doctors to identify quickly which patients were affected when the popular arthritis medication Vioxx was recalled. The VHA's integrated system of tracking and diagnosis is saving lives.

Developed at taxpayers' expense, the VHA software program is now available for free and is currently being used by public health care systems in Finland, Germany, Egypt, and Nigeria. Yet officials say they are unaware of any private health care system in the United States that has adopted the software. Why? As Lawrence Casalino, a professor of public health at the University of Chicago, puts it, "The U.S. medical market as presently constituted simply does not provide a strong business case for quality." Translated, that means quality health care is not profitable, so big health care corporations aren't interested.[10] The VHA's success shows that Americans clearly could have higher-quality health care at lower cost. Ironically, it's a government bureaucracy that's setting the health care standard, and it's the private sector that's lagging behind.

Another instructive example of smart government is in the area of affordable housing. Affordable housing for the poorest and neediest Americans has been a challenge for every administration. Public housing from the 1960s War on Poverty programs became ghettoized, crime-ridden high-rises concentrated on the outskirts of cities. By the early 1990s, the Republican solution was to sell off public housing to the impoverished tenants, an early example of the "ownership society." But saddling poor tenants, many of whom had trouble managing their personal lives, with the responsibility for maintaining decrepit high-rise buildings in terrible neighborhoods turned out to be a losing, though well-meaning, proposition.[11]

The Clinton administration, guided by Secretary of Housing and Urban Development Henry Cisneros, figured out a better strategy, combining a mix of traditionally Democratic and Republican solutions. Cisneros broke up that concentrated poverty by tearing down the public housing complexes and encouraging the building of low-rise replacement public housing in different parts of the city. Smartly, he also implemented choice-enhancing, market-based tactics long favored by Republicans and disparaged by Democrats. He gave departing residents Section 8 housing vouchers to help them find private apartments in better neighborhoods. He also provided tax credits to private and nonprofit developers to build or rehab apartment buildings, with rules requiring that they rent to a mix of both poor and working-class tenants. Cisneros's policies reflected one of the formulas of smart government: empowering individuals by creating more choices (with housing vouchers) through precisely targeted government regulation (providing tax credits to developers for building more housing) to break up concentrated, ghettoized poverty. Paul Glastris, editor of *Washington Monthly*, writes that "these largely unsung efforts helped drive the renewal of many urban centers that took place in the 1990s. Surveys by the Urban Institute show that those who left public housing did wind up in somewhat better neighborhoods."[12]

These are just a few examples of smart government in action. In many areas, smart government can outperform the private sector, such as in health care, or it can cajole the private sector, such as by creating medical insurance pools for small businesses or tax credits for low-income housing developers. Political leaders interested in restoring Americans' faith in government should look for ways to make government credible, worthy, and smart in the minds of the American people.

Yet, as we have seen, even when government does good things, it does not receive the recognition it deserves. How many people would have guessed that the Veterans Health Administration is providing the best health care in America by making extensive use of electronic medical records and information technology? Or that low-income, government-funded housing has made gains in sheltering a very difficult and needy population? Why don't Americans know that? The answer is simple: because no one has told them. The profit-mad media do not report it because they are too invested in "if it bleeds, it leads" journalism to boost their audience share, and positive stories don't make bold headlines. And conservatives don't want the public to know about it. In fact, a leading business magazine that had commissioned an article on America's health care practices decided to kill the story when the research showed the government-run veterans hospitals as the best.

BRAGGING ABOUT GOVERNMENT

Part of the solution to counteract this antigovernment ideology is simply a matter of better communication to the public about the good that government does. It's a public relations challenge that needs to be waged. But how? We can learn something from the government of Sweden. During a recent trip to Stockholm and other Swedish cities, I saw advertisements in the commuter trains and buses that said, "Your Health Care System: Working for You." The government-run health care system was advertising and promoting its services and accomplishments. There were other ads similarly advertising other accomplishments of the Swedish government, which has fostered one of the most competitive economies in the world at the same time it provides a premium health and social care systems.

So part of the solution is to use old-fashioned, conventional means: product advertisement. Just as any business knows, advertising is essential to marketing and branding your product.

Government should advertise its accomplishments just like a business does through TV and radio ads, reminding the public of the good things it accomplishes. Corporations do this; why shouldn't government? A potential advertising theme could be "Government Is Good for You," with the ads showing the many ways that government does good things for individuals and communities, from providing direct services to producing regulations that facilitate business providing direct services. Imagine ads showing the volume of mail moved every day through the U.S. Postal Service; the scientific breakthroughs funded by government; the transportation and communication advances fostered by government. How about an ad extolling the virtues of the 40-hour workweek, and paid vacations and holidays to spend time with your family, all legislated by the government? How about an ad showing the breathtaking beauty of America's national parks, or ads showing the growth of home ownership resulting from mortgage and interest rate policies, all established by the government? Or ads illustrating the government lending a hand to people struck by natural disasters, or personal life disasters and medical emergencies?

Yes, in all these areas and more, government has done a lot. Government should have clear bragging rights over big business or corporations, yet government never does the bragging. It's the unsung hero. Compare those sorts of positive ads to the constant negative litany coming from the right, and even from many Democrats, running down government and echoing Reagan that government is the problem, despite so much evidence to the contrary.

Such advertisement also would prod Americans to reflect on the proper role of government in the "practical management of a modern economy." That discussion would prompt a dialogue about who should benefit from that economy and answer JFK's questions about how to eradicate the barriers to education and employment as well as how to provide "adequate profits for enterprise, adequate wages for labor, and opportunity for all." If one of the consequences of Hurricane Katrina is that Americans reevaluate our views of government, that would be a welcome silver lining, an overdue turning in American politics.

▍ Summary of Recommendations

1. Promote "smart government" rather than "limited government" or "big government."
2. Government should use conventional means of TV and radio advertising to remind Americans of the many good things that government does, past and present.

Conclusion

Renewing the American Republic

No single, magical solution will, by itself, remake American democracy. Seen in isolation, each democratic breakdown appears as little more than the occasional squeaks of our political system. But when juxtaposed together, like the pieces of a jigsaw puzzle, that's when a broader picture emerges of an overall corrosion that is steadily weakening our republic. And that's why the reforms proposed in this book are designed to form a coherent picture, an overall vision, of what we need our republic to look like in the future. By glimpsing this big picture, we also can see why the weakening of our republic is not coincidental. Rather, it's the result of a long-standing political struggle, with deep philosophical roots, about the nature of American democracy and the role of government.

On one side of this struggle are those who see representative democracy as a vehicle for self-government and popular endowment. This is a strong current in the American stream, propelled forward by the likes of Jefferson, Madison, Lincoln, Susan B. Anthony, Thurgood Marshall, Martin Luther King and many others, each in their own time and way. On the other side are those who believe in an elite democracy that requires only occasional popular input and ratification, this too is a strong current in the American stream. Richard Nixon typified the latter attitude when he stated "blacks, whites, Mexicans and the rest" shouldn't have anything to say about government "because they don't have the brains to know." But Nixon's attitude is the 200-years-later version of the one stated by John Jay and other founders when Jay said that the upper classes "were the better kind of people" and that "the people who own the country ought to govern it." The Framers put a short leash on what they saw as "too much democracy" and burdened us with an unrepresentative Senate and the Electoral College as a way to contain the popular will. They were suspicious of "we the people," and the consequences of their decisions still affect us today.

George W. Bush's "ownership society" is the latest apotheosis of this political philosophy of elite rule yet, ironically, it portrays itself as the most democratic of policies, centered on a philosophy of individual freedom. Amid all the sound bites, it is easy to forget that, if individual freedom is the primary goal, then the greatest amount of freedom can be found in a state of nature where the strongest, the fastest, and the fiercest prevail. Yet in that situation one person's freedom can be another's tyranny. The march of human history is about doing better than the law of the jungle—it is about the human species learning to live and work together in order to make things better for all and cleverly devising institutions that make that possible. The current Republican leadership seems determined to unlearn all that.

The recent resurgence of antidemocratic attitudes makes it more urgent than ever that, as a nation, we reengage with a fundamental question: Does the American way of life require a participatory democracy and an engaged citizenry, like Alexis de Tocqueville observed here in the 1830s when he wrote, "The political activity that pervades the United States must be seen in order to be understood. No sooner do you set foot on American ground then you are stunned by a kind of tumult"?[1] Or can our nation exist, as conservative columnists Charles Krauthammer and George Will have suggested, as a "check-off" democracy, where most citizens live their lives mostly ignoring politics, rising up at the ballot box only when riled by grossly offensive government policy, repugnant behavior by a politician, or an external threat? According to Krauthammer, "Low voter turnout is a leading indicator of contentment."[2] But this claim ignores reams of evidence about who does and who does not vote. Non-voters are overwhelmingly racial minority, less affluent, or younger than those who vote. In other words, those who have the *least* reason to be satisfied are those who are no-shows on Election Day.

As tempting as may be the vision of a democracy that runs on aristocratic autopilot, the reality is that an elite, trickle-down political system eventually dead-ends in arrogance, secretiveness, and abuse of power. History is filled with examples of this bitter lesson, from the Roman Republic's prototype democracy dominated by wealthy elites that eventually imploded into Caesar's dictatorship, to Germany's Weimar Republic that transmogrified into the brutality of Hitler's Third Reich.[3] Will the American Republic suffer a similar fate?

Many Republican leaders today seem to share the views of Nixon, Krauthammer, and the most aristocratic of the Founders on representative democracy and governance. They argue that "government is the problem" and therefore should be kept as small as possible (at least when it comes to social programs, though not, apparently, military budgets). Government is not supposed to do much for you; instead, it is supposed to get out of the way and let a nation of rugged individualists fend for themselves. Though many Republicans don't care much anymore for Charles Darwin's ideas about evolution, they sure seem to like social Darwinism and an elite society based on the survival of the fittest—they call it "the ownership society." Their stated goal is to support democracy around the world, but a truly representative democracy in the United States is the last thing they want because it's likely that a more robust, representative system would choose to unshackle government to do more for average Americans.

But the Democratic Party has not been much better. Democrats, who in the late 20th century were the party of the New Deal and extending fundamental civil rights to more Americans, have lost their way and mostly stopped pushing for a truly representative or even functioning democracy. And since Bill Clinton declared "the era of big government is over," the Democratic Party has been unable to articulate either a popular role for government or even a reason for their party's existence, except as non-Republicans. As I write these lines, Democrats control the governor's office and both houses of the state legislature in eight states; in seven more, they control both legislative chambers with fairly moderate Republican governors.[4] In many or all of these states, the Democrats could seize the initiative to enact most of the political reforms proposed in this book. Will they? In my experience, most elected Democrats seem, at best, only dimly aware of the problems, much less the solutions. They seem to think that whatever rules elected them must be fine and that Democrats' loss of political power to the Republicans is only temporary, so steady-on. They have been saying this now for over 10 years.

It is little wonder, then, that American democracy has been working about as well as the levees around New Orleans. Neither the ruling party nor the opposition seems to value our representative democracy, our history of engaged struggle to improve this 18th-century invention or, ultimately, government itself. And the American people, especially young people and minorities, have turned away in droves. The rest of the world is shaking its head and wondering what to do about this lone remaining superpower, armed to the teeth, which seems to be descending into an era of post-democracy.

A TALE OF TWO FUTURES

What will be the future of representative democracy in the United States? America is standing at a fork in the road, staring into the distance of an unknown landscape. Allow me to present two possible alternatives.

Imagine that it is Election Day 2016. Imagine yet another presidential election that boils down to the same two battleground states—Ohio and Florida—which is not unrealistic, given current demographic trends. Candidates will spend most of their time in these two states and perhaps a handful of other swing states, ignoring all the others. Visits to our largest states (e.g., California, Texas, New York) will be only to fund-raising mother lodes and select ZIP codes. Florida and Ohio electorates will be sliced and diced into bite-sized targets at which will be aimed carefully crafted campaign missiles. Ohioans and Floridians will be carpet bombed with television ads, most of them negative, making television virtually unwatchable for the final 30 days of the campaign, while in the rest of the nation it will be all quiet on the electoral front.

In a close race, spoiler candidates still will threaten to wreck the majority mandate of the front-runners, perplexing voters with "lesser of two evils" dilemmas and acting as a damper on new candidates and their ideas. All campaign spin and hype will be directed toward the narrowest slices of voters, either the partisan base or undecided swing voters, which will determine the winner. Consequently, the nation's most important election mostly will be dumbed down to a handful of parochial issues, as all the other issues facing the nation—and the voters who care about them—will watch the election as if spectators from the 42th row.

In this 2016 presidential election, unfortunately, we never did fix the problems with election administration and voting equipment, so out of 120 million voters nationwide, a change of only a few thousand or perhaps even a few hundred votes in either Ohio or Florida—whether by administrative miscues or fraud—can alter the outcome. Further complicating matters is that, with the numbers of minorities in the electorate rising every year, some conservative organizations have increased efforts to use various tricks to disenfranchise minorities. In 2015, a few states, including Florida, even tried passing English-language requirements for voters—and nearly succeeded. The roller coaster of the 2016 electoral season already has resulted in dozens of lawsuits in Florida, Ohio, and across the nation, ensuring that no matter which side wins, the nation once again will lose.

Not only that, but congressional districts have continued their plummet into one-party fiefdoms. In the 2016 congressional elections, only 10 out of 435 district races are even remotely competitive. To its credit, Congress passed a national law in 2011 outlawing partisan gerrymandering and mandating independent redistricting commissions in all states—yet it had very little impact. Republican and Democratic voters have become so bunkered down into their own red and blue regions that the line-drawing process mostly has become inconsequential. To counteract that, reformers managed to pass clean money/full public financing in a dozen states by 2014, a tremendous accomplishment—yet with so many red and blue winner-take-all districts dominating the political landscape, that success also has made little difference in terms of who gets elected or the policies they pass, though it has introduced some badly needed political debate into our brain-dead elections.

The House finally passed legislation guaranteeing health care for all Americans via a government–private sector joint effort, but senators representing a mere 15 percent of the nation's population were able to kill it. The senators from these low-population states were concerned about an expansion of big government, even though their own states are heavily subsidized by the federal government, receiving twice as many federal tax dollars as they pay out and three times the per capita federal dollars received by California.

Yet, despite all the partisan pyrotechnics and passion on both sides, hardly anyone is going to show up to vote on Election Day 2016. Disgusted by the partisan sandbox play, and the hyperpartisan media, and a government so out of touch with the concerns of average Americans, voters continued their trend of staying home. The fact is, most voters no longer need to show up since most races are decided well in advance of Election Day, and so they don't bother—voter turnout for congressional races plunged to barely a quarter of eligible voters in 2014. In recent years, cities such as Dallas, Charlotte, Austin, New York, Boston, and others have seen voter turnout for mayoral elections in the single digits. In one recent mayoral race in Los Angeles, only 5 percent of eligible voters could be bothered to interrupt their busy Tuesday—a workday, after all—to cast a vote.

Some pundits have begun to wonder out loud on editorial pages and talking-head shows, Do elections even matter anymore? Not only has turnout continued to plunge, but certain cities in California canceled their elections because there were no candidates to compete against the safe-seat incumbents. In fact, the Howard Jarvis Taxpayers Association, which has raised a public ruckus over the cost of elections where so few voters show up, has begun collecting signatures on a California initiative that will cancel elections except for one election every eight years. In essence, the Howard Jarvisites are asking the few remaining voters to permanently cancel most elections and transmogrify the United States into a "ratification" democracy with occasional elections and referendums, more like the plutocratic Roman Republic than a participatory democratic republic. And polls show the ballot measure has a good chance of passing.

The onset of this post-democratic future has paved the way for the "Berlusconization" of American politics. Silvio Berlusconi is the Italian media magnate and political patriarch who managed to gobble up nearly all private media in Italy, and then he used that resource as a personal stepping stone to political domination in 2000. By 2016, the trajectory of America's shattered democracy has moved us a giant step closer to a Berlusconi-type figure lurking on the horizon—Newt Gingrich, who in an alliance with Rupert Murdoch and Clear Channel, has returned to the spotlight and launched his late entry into the presidential campaign, backed by Murdoch's and Clear Channel's media empire of Fox News and thousands of local radio and TV broadcasters and daily newspapers across the United States. Gingrich is strongly playing the national security card, popular among certain voters concerned about the ongoing War on Terror, now in its 15th year. Gingrich's polling numbers quickly surge into the high 30s, making him the front-runner and throwing all calculations about the race into a tizzy.

On Election Day 2016, America takes a big gulp and prepares for a grim outcome. There is to be no winner in a country so bedeviled by bitter partisanship and antiquated political institutions and practices. The rest of the world can only watch and shake their heads in disbelief, a by-now familiar posture toward the former leader of the Western world. This is the way American democracy ends, not with a bang but with a whimper.

Instead of a gloomy future of post-democracy, another future is possible—one of renewed democracy. Imagine a different election in 2016, one where all 190 million eligible voters, including the millions of minority and young voters, have been automatically registered to vote as a result of a federal law passed in 2014 enacting universal voter registration. Imagine that law also signed up the United States into the ranks of other advanced democracies that have lifted all barriers to participation, including allowing residents of our nation's capital to participate fully and elect congressional representation; allowing our poorest citizens to vote on equipment as good as the wealthy county next door; and allowing prisoners to become inculcated in the good habits of citizenship while incarcerated, including the basic act of voting. This federal law enfranchising all of these new voters amounted to the greatest civil rights advance since 1965 and dramatically changed the profile of the electorate.

Imagine that, in 2011, Congress finally passed a law ensuring that voting equipment and election administration would be overseen by a national elections commission that rigorously tests and produces the best voting equipment and election administrative practices, partnering with states, counties, and the private sector to ensure that every corner of America is technologically equipped and trained to count our ballots accurately and securely. Election officials are now trained and certified professionals, with expertise in computer technology, databases, the logistics of running elections, and public relations.

By the 2016 presidential election, 21 states have signed presidential election treaties awarding all their state's electoral votes to the winner of the national popular vote, enough that the election has become a de facto direct election for president. Candidates no longer can confine their campaigns to a handful of battleground states, especially the bigger ones such as Ohio and Florida. Instead, the candidates crisscross the nation, ignoring practically no one, trying to pick up every single vote they can. In 2016, it's going to be a close race, just as it has been in every presidential election since 2000, and no one knows whether the decisive votes will come from Wyoming, North Dakota, Georgia, California, or some other state. This in turn leads to a massive mobilization of voters, old and new, who suddenly aren't being treated like spectators anymore or ignored because they happen to live in the wrong state.

These 21 states as well as several others also have decided to use instant runoff voting (IRV) to guarantee majority winners, so the presence of several independent and third party candidates not only doesn't split the vote or spoil the race, but in fact injects new ideas and fresh faces into the race that excites more voters. Suddenly voters can hear a range of candidates directly addressing their concerns. And they can vote for these candidates without shooting themselves in the foot and contributing to their least favorite candidate winning. The net effect of this national direct election using IRV in many states is that voter turnout in the 2016 presidential race surges across the nation to a phenomenal 77 percent of eligible voters, on a par with many other democracies, and the highest turnout in more than 120 years.

But that's not all. By 2016, imagine that 19 states have scrapped their antiquated winner-take-all elections and adopted proportional representation for electing their state legislatures and congressional delegation. As a result, multiparty democracies have sprouted in all these states, giving voters a whole new range of independent candidates and political parties to choose from. Not only Democrats and Republicans, but also a Libertarian Party, a Green Party, a Working Families Party, and a centrist Ross Perot–type New America Party are all vying for legislative seats. The candidates for the different parties are funded by public financing and free media time, so even the smaller parties have sufficient resources to reach voters with TV and radio ads about their platforms and policy proposals. The result is real free market competition in our elections. For the first time in their lives, millions of voters are hearing a genuine debate with a full range of policy choices. Voters feel more informed and more satisfied with their political choices across the political spectrum. As a result, voter turnout for state and congressional elections has doubled in many of these states to an average of 70 percent of eligible voters, nearly as high as many other nations. Other states also are beginning to take steps to scrap their winner-take-all systems in favor of the more advanced proportional methods.

A few years earlier, in 2013, the U.S. Senate finally was recognized as the 18th-century anachronism it is, but political resistance from low-population states that benefit most from this unrepresentative body meant that reform possibilities were limited. Nevertheless, the Twenty-eighth Amendment to the Constitution was passed in 2015, greatly reducing the Senate's powers, taking away its power to confirm Supreme Court justices and other presidential appointments, transforming it into an upper chamber like that in other advanced democracies that can delay legislation initiated by the House, but not stop it or introduce its own legislation.

With the Senate scaled back, reform seems to be in the air, leading to moves to overhaul the Supreme Court. Another constitutional amendment has been passed by Congress and sent to the states for ratification that will employ 15-year judicial term limits, multiple appointing authorities, and a mandatory retirement age of 75. If passed by three-fourths of the states, the Twenty-ninth Amendment will ensure that the Supreme Court becomes, for the first time in decades, a balance of legal-political views that better reflects the views of most Americans.

With broader representation in Congress and many of the state legislatures—including perspectives from the right, left, and center—policy adjusts so that it aligns more closely with the opinions of most Americans. Congress passes sensible laws to regulate the corporate media, forcing Big Media to sign a legally binding charter with detailed requirements for how they are going to serve the public interest, including adequate news coverage and free airtime for all candidates. Cable companies finally are brought to heel and made to serve the public interest, with a regulated pricing structure and cooperative agreements with cities and rural areas to bring broadband Internet access to all citizens, even the poorest. The Fairness Doctrine has been restored, ensuring that all sides and opinions can be heard, reducing the inclination of Americans to bunker down in their own impoverished media ghettos.

Public broadcasting has been granted robust funding to nearly European-type levels via a small mandatory monthly fee, and daily newspapers are being subsidized, resulting in a flowering of dailies. Newspapers even are incorporated into classrooms, getting high school students into the habit of reading the news. With more robust public and private media, the result has been a surge of interest and knowledge by Americans in news and politics, and an improvement in the quality of political discourse and citizenship, leading to new understanding and respect among Americans of differing viewpoints.

The cumulative effect of all these changes by Election Day 2016 is that, in so many ways, the winner-take-all mentality— the adversarial "if I win, you lose" mantra—has begun to transform. Whether it's in the legislatures, the executive branch, the media, or the courts, a new form of consensual democracy is emerging where various points of view compete against each other in a more respectful manner, sometimes strongly disagreeing but no longer crossing the line between vigorous advocacy and bitter "win at all costs" partisanship. In such a climate of multipartisan collegiality, where the collective mind-set can come together and share perspectives in order to craft compromises and solutions for the good of the nation, Congress is able to chart a legislative course for America's future, including figuring out a plan to ensure that every American has health care, cradle to grave, and a decent retirement too, using a mix of public-private partnerships.

With legislative chambers functioning more as pragmatic, deliberative, problem-solving bodies instead of the mud-wrestling pits of partisan warfare, Americans no longer are so frustrated by paralyzed politics and stop looking to millionaire politicians or poorly crafted voter initiatives to fix the mess. Government acquires a better reputation. Americans see that smart government—not big government or "cut to the bone" government—can assist them in living prosperous, healthy, and enjoyable lives without overly restricting their liberty or freedoms. Once again America presents a more cooperative leadership on the world's stage, much to the world's relief. All of this ushers in a new era of shared prosperity among all Americans, and the rising tide helps lift boats the world over.

This is one alternative future for the United States. Down this path lies a renewal of American democracy that will allow our nation to live up to the lofty rhetoric of our Founders' homily— "We the People, in Order to form a more perfect Union . . . ." A renewed democracy will create a nation that works for all of us, instead of some of us. But down another path—much like the current path, relying on antiquated institutions and practices— lies a downward spiral into post-democracy, a nightmarish future where political and economic cabals wielding ominous technology have hog-tied democracy, turning our nation into one that works for only a handful of us, instead of all of us. These are two very different alternative futures, founded on two very different philosophies regarding representative democracy—elite rule versus popular sovereignty. We are standing at a fork in the road, and the choice is ours.

AMERICAN DEMOCRACY IN THE 21ST CENTURY

Like the rest of the world, the United States must adapt to profound political and economic changes that are sweeping the globe. The reforms proposed in this book are meant to bring the American political economy into the 21st century and foster a more participatory democracy and engaged citizenry that in turn will produce government that better reflects the priorities of the American people. Those who think America is best served by an elite democracy with a disengaged citizenry will oppose these reforms. But those who believe our collective future requires more engagement, better representation, and better government should fight for these reforms with all their might, for as long as it takes.

Those striving for a more democratic republic will find several positives working in our favor. Many political leaders, old and new, Republican and Democrat—including John McCain, Jim Leach, Jimmy Carter, Barack Obama, Howard Dean, Orrin Hatch, Tom Campbell, Hillary Clinton, Dianne Feinstein, even James Baker—have supported various reforms proposed in this book. And new leadership will arise among young people that is less attached to the flypaper of old ideas. For example, two dozen universities—including Harvard, Stanford, MIT, Duke, Princeton, UCLA, Cal-Berkeley, and others—currently use either instant runoff voting or proportional representation to elect their student governments, helping create a generation of future leaders who have familiarity with advanced electoral systems.

Moreover, in the age of the Internet, more Americans are learning about advanced democratic methods being used in other nations and in some parts of the United States that are superior to our antiquated methods.

Perhaps most important, time is on our side. America will change because it has to. As bad as our dreary politics seem now, imagine the situation 10 or 15 years further down the road toward post-democracy. With our national racial demographics continuing to shift, and as our democratic breakdowns attract more attention and our country continues to decline, momentum for reform will increase. Understandably, many people look at the political landscape today and throw up their hands, concluding things will never change. But how many Germans in 1980 thought the Berlin Wall would fall in less than 10 years? I have spoken to many Germans who in 1988 did not think the Berlin Wall would fall less than a year later. The take-home lesson is that you never know at any given moment where you stand on the fault lines of political evolution. Change proceeds very slowly, via inch-by-inch movements of the tectonic plates, until suddenly they are unleashed in an earthquake of unexpected proportions. A similar process is occurring in the United States today.

So despite the seeming odds, we urgently need to press forward with efforts focused on adopting the reforms proposed in this book. Everybody can do a little, volunteering time and resources to the various organizations listed at the end of each chapter. Paraphrasing Milton Friedman, we need to develop political alternatives and "keep them alive and available" until the "politically impossible becomes politically inevitable." That day is approaching, and the stakes couldn't be higher. One step at a time we will transform the American political system, taking it out of the 18th-century museum in which it is stuck and transplanting it into the 21st century.

Notes

INTRODUCTION

1. Confusion exists over the terms *republic* and *democracy*, with some people saying, "The United States is a republic, not a democracy," which is incorrect. A *republic* is a form of democracy where laws are passed by democratically elected representatives (as opposed to a *direct democracy*, where average citizens are empowered to pass laws, such as in New England town meetings). A republic is a subbranch of the greater tree trunk of "democracy," making the United States both a republic *and* a democracy. To clarify this confusion, I frequently use *representative democracy* interchangeably with *republic*.

2. Milton Friedman, *Capitalism and Freedom* (Chicago: University of Chicago Press, 1962), preface.

3. Voting records in Congress show more legislators consistently voting with their party than ever before. See Isaiah J. Poole, "Party Unity Vote Study: Votes Echo Electoral Themes," *Congressional Quarterly Weekly*, December 11, 2004, 2906-8; and Jeffrey McMurray, "Conservative Southern Dems Disappearing," Associated Press, April 25, 2005.

4. Ted Halstead and Michael Lind, *The Radical Center* (New York: Anchor Books, 2002), 3.

5. The Gallup poll, conducted January 25–26, 2000, is cited in Halstead and Lind, *The Radical Center*, 229, n. 1. Also see John Avalon, "Independent President in 2008?" *New York Sun*, June 14, 2005; and Richard Winger, *Ballot Access News* 20, no. 8 (December 1, 2004): 3, chart.

6. Halstead and Lind, *The Radical Center*, 111–12.

7. See the Zogby poll released June 30, 2005, "No Bounce: Bush Job Approval Unchanged by War Speech; Question on Impeachment Shows Polarization of Nation; Americans Tired of Divisiveness in Congress—Want Bi-Partisan Solutions," http://www.zogby.com/news/ReadNews.dbm?ID=1007.

8. "Newspaper: Butterfly Ballot Cost Gore White House," *CNN.com*, March 11, 2001, http://archives.cnn.com/2001/ALLPOLITICS/03/11/palmbeach.recount/. CNN reported that the *Palm Beach Post*'s review of discarded butterfly ballots found Gore lost 6,607 votes when voters marked more than one name on the confusing ballot.

9. See National Research Commission on Elections and Voting, "Interim Report on Alleged Irregularities in the United States Presidential Election of 2 November 2004," December 22, 2004, http://elections.ssrc.org. Also see National Research Commission on Elections and Voting, "Panel of the Nation's Top Elections Scholars Finds No Proof of Fraud in 2004 Presidential Vote," press release, December 2004.
10. Jimmy Carter, "Still Seeking a Fair Florida Vote," *Washington Post*, September 27, 2004, A19.
11. See the 2002 report by Institute for Democracy and Electoral Assistance, "Voter Turnout since 1945: A Global Report," 84. This figure is for parliamentary (i.e., congressional elections—not presidential elections), which averaged 47.7 percent of the voting age population in the United States during the post–World War II era.
12. For example, see John Cochran, "A Government Out of Touch," *Congressional Quarterly Weekly*, July 4, 2005, 1804. Also see Steven Hill, *Fixing Elections: The Failure of America's Winner Take All Politics* (New York: Routledge, 2002), vii; 305, nn. 1–8.
13. Howard Kurtz, "The Spinners, Casting Their Versions of the Vote in Iraq," *Washington Post*, February 1, 2005, C01. Also see the website of FairVote: The Center for Voting and Democracy, at http://www.fairvote.org.
14. One study of 2000 U.S. House elections showed a marked decline in voter turnout among the least competitive races, by as much as 19 points. See Center for Voting and Democracy, "Dubious Democracy 2001," http://www.fairvote.org/?page=199. In the 2004 presidential election, voter turnout rose 9 percent—to 63 percent—in the 12 most competitive states, but only 2 percent—to 53 percent—in the 12 least competitive states. Voter turnout among 18- to 29-year-olds was 64.4 percent in the 10 most competitive states and 47.6 percent in the remaining states—a gap of 17 percent. See FairVote, "The Shrinking Battleground: The 2008 Presidential Elections and Beyond," http://www.fairvote.org/whopicks/?page=1555.
15. Interestingly, the GOP gerrymanders in these five states alone give the Republicans most of their 15-seat majority in the House. In Michigan, Pennsylvania, Florida, and Ohio, the Republicans and Democrats are essentially tied, statewide (Democrats recently have won presidential, gubernatorial, and/or U.S. Senate statewide votes in Michigan, Pennsylvania, and Florida, and Kerry barely lost Ohio to Bush as Ohio Democrats won 49 percent of the ag-

gregate statewide vote for U.S. House races). Yet the Republicans won two-thirds of the U.S. House seats in those four states (51 out of 77 races), mostly as a result of GOP-drawn districts. In Texas, Republicans won 58 percent of the aggregate statewide vote for U.S. House races but 66 percent of the seats. If the "votes to seats" imbalances in these five states were corrected, Democrats would pick up about 14 seats, narrowing the GOP majority in the House to one vote.

16. John Adams, *Thoughts on Government: Applicable to the Present State of the American Colonies* (Philadelphia: John Dunlap, 1776). Adams's view was fairly common among the Framers and Founders; see Hannah Pitkin, *The Concept of Representation* (Berkeley: University of California Press, 1967), 60–61.

17. Following the 2004 elections, the U.S. House of Representatives had 64 women representatives out of 435 (14.7 percent) and 68 racial minorities (40 blacks, 25 Hispanics, and 3 Asians—15.6 percent).

18. See Mildred L. Amer, "Membership of the 109th Congress: A Profile," CRS Report for Congress, May 31, 2005, http://www .senate.gov/reference/resources/pdf/RS22007.pdf. This report shows 160 representatives listing their occupation as law and 163 citing business (though members often list more than one profession when surveyed by Congressional Quarterly, Inc.).

19. Bill O'Reilly made this remark during an interview on Jon Stewart's *The Daily Show with Jon Stewart* on Comedy Central.

20. Thomas B. Edsall and Derek Willis, "Fundraising Records Broken by Both Major Political Parties," *Washington Post*, December 3, 2004, A07.

21. David S. Broder, "Jerry Ford's Sense," *Washington Post*, June 16, 1999, A37.

22. Eric Schmitt, "Military Admits Planting News in Iraq," *New York Times*, December 3, 2005.

23. "The Times and Iraq," *New York Times*, May 26, 2004 (though the *Times*'s apology appeared on p. A10 instead of on the front page where many of Miller's stories had appeared).

24. Peter Johnson, "Amanpour: CNN Practiced Self-Censorship," *USA Today*, September 15, 2003.

25. See Program on International Policy Attitudes (PIPA), "The Federal Budget: The Public's Priorities," March 7, 2005, http://www.pipa .org/OnlineReports/budget/030705/Report03_07_05.pdf. PIPA is a joint program of the University of Maryland's Center on Policy Attitudes and the Center for International and Security Studies.

The poll was conducted February 18–25, 2005, with a nationwide sample of 1,182 American adults.

26. Christopher Swann, "More Americans Lack Cover for Ill-Health," *Financial Times*, August 30, 2005. Also see David Leonhardt, "U.S. Poverty Rate Rose in 2004, Even as Economy Grew," *New York Times/International Herald Tribune*, September 1, 2005.

27. Associated Press, "Growing Debt and the Doomsday Scenario," *St. Petersburg Times*, September 4, 2005. For the first time in history, total household debts surpassed total after-tax incomes, a precarious level not even reached pre-1929.

28. David Wessel, "As Rich-Poor Gap Widens in the U.S., Class Mobility Stalls," *Wall Street Journal*, May 13, 2005, A1. Also see "Middle of the Class," *The Economist*, July 14, 2005.

29. John Cochran, "A Government Out of Touch," *Congressional Quarterly Weekly*, July 4, 2005, 1804.

30. This conversation was tape-recorded by Nixon's own hidden surveillance system that he had installed in the Oval Office. James Warren, "Some Vintage Nixon Saves the Day," *Chicago Tribune*, August 19, 2001.

31. See Richard A. Posner, *Law, Pragmatism, and Democracy* (Cambridge, MA: Harvard University Press, 2003).

32. Jerry Fresia, *Toward an American Revolution: Exposing the Constitution and Other Illusions* (Boston: South End, 1988), 32.

CHAPTER 1

1. Portions of this chapter were drawn from my article "10 Steps to Better Elections," *Sierra*, May/June 2005, 46–50.

2. Guy Gugliotta, "Study Finds Millions of Votes Lost," *Washington Post*, July 17, 2001, A1. Also see the press release dated July 16, 2001, from the Voting Technology Project, a comprehensive Caltech-MIT study initiated after the November election debacle, http://vote.caltech.edu.

3. Adam Liptak, "Voting Problems in Ohio Set Off an Alarm," *New York Times*, November 7, 2004; *USA Today*, "Election Day Leftovers," December 27, 2004, editorial.

4. Michael Powell and Peter Slevin, "Several Factors Contributed to 'Lost' Voters in Ohio," *Washington Post*, December 15, 2004, A1. Unlike those in many other states, Ohio election officials decided only to count provisional ballots cast in the precise precinct in

which the voter lived, ignoring the spirit of the federal law that established a right to vote a provisional ballot for any voter who, for whatever reason, is not on the voter rolls. That ballot is supposed to be researched to figure out whether the voter is eligible; if so, the ballot is supposed to be counted.

5. Powell and Slevin, "Several Factors Contributed to 'Lost' Voters in Ohio," A1.

6. Christopher Hitchens, "Ohio's Odd Numbers," *Vanity Fair*, March 2005.

7. Paul Krugman, "What They Did Last Fall," *New York Times*, August 19, 2005.

8. "Untangling the Voting Controversies," *Cleveland Plain-Dealer*, December 5, 2005, http://www.cleveland.com/news/wide/index.ssf?/politics/conspiracies.html; Hitchens, "Ohio's Odd Numbers."

9. Powell and Slevin, "Several Factors Contributed to 'Lost' Voters in Ohio," A1.

10. Dennis J. Willard and Doug Oplinger, "Ohio Counties Have More Registrations Than Voters; Fraud Not Necessarily Cause," *Akron Beacon Journal*, October 2, 2004, A8. The four counties and their 2004 vote for Bush were Franklin, 45 percent; Delaware, 66 percent; Fayette, 63 percent; and Mercer, 75 percent.

11. Michael Moss, "Big G.O.P. Bid to Challenge Voters at Polls in Key State," *New York Times*, October 23, 2004.

12. Ann Louise Bardach, "How Florida Republicans Keep Blacks from Voting," *Los Angeles Times*, September 26, 2004.

13. BBC News, "Florida Ballot Papers Go Missing," October 28, 2004, http://news.bbc.co.uk/1/hi/world/americas/3960679.stm.

14. See Institute for Policy Studies, "Obstacles to a Democratic Election: Reports of Electoral Problems in Key U.S. States during the 2004 Election," November 2004, pp. 3, 5, 7, and 11; Alan Elsner, "Millions Blocked from Voting in U.S. Election," Reuters, September 22, 2004.

15. For details on voting irregularities across the United States, see the website of FairVote, specifically, http://www.fairvote.org/?page=72.

16. Keith Ervin and Susan Gilmore, "Judge Blocks Count of Newly Discovered Ballots," *Seattle Times*, December 17, 2004.

17. Triad Systems is owned by a man named Tod Rapp, who has donated money to the Republican National Committee, the Ohio Republican Party State Central & Executive Committee, the National Republican Congressional Committee, the George W. Bush

reelection campaign, and a GOP candidate for Senate. Data provided by the Federal Elections Commission.

18. John Nolan, "Return of the Hanging Chad: Recount Continues in Ohio," *Boston Globe*, December 16, 2004; Kim Zetter, "Ohio Recount Stirs Trouble," *Wired.com*, December 20, 2004.

19. See National Research Commission on Elections and Voting, "Interim Report on Alleged Irregularities in the United States Presidential Election of 2 November 2004," December 22, 2004, http://elections.ssrc.org; also see "Panel of the Nation's Top Elections Scholars Finds No Proof of Fraud in 2004 Presidential Vote," press release from the National Research Commission on Elections and Voting, December 2004.

20. Erik Lazarus stated this in his presentation to the Voting Systems Testing Summit, November 28–29, 2005, Sacramento, California, organized by California's secretary of state.

21. Geri Smith, "Election Lessons from Mexico," *Business Week*, November 2, 2004.

22. In 2001, Ciber, Inc., gave $25,000 to the Republican National Committee/Republican National State Elections Committee and also $23,000 to a Republican candidate for U.S. Senate, Wayne Allard, who is now a sitting senator from Colorado. In total, Ciber employees and spouses donated more than $72,000 to GOP candidates and groups during 2001–2004, and Wyle Laboratories gave $5,750, all of it to Republican candidates, according to the Center for Responsive Politics. Source: Federal Elections Commission data, found on http://www.opensecrets.org; and Roger Fillion, "Workers at Voting Firm Gave to GOP," *Rocky Mountain News*, August 21, 2004.

23. "On the Voting Machine Makers' Tab," *New York Times*, September 12, 2004, editorial.

24. Tim Reiterman and Peter Nicholas, "Ex-Officials Now behind New Voting Machines," *Los Angeles Times*, November 10, 2003.

25. Paul R. La Monica, "The Trouble with e-voting," CNN/*Money*, August 30, 2004, http://money.cnn.com/2004/08/30/technology/ election_diebold/; Andrew Kantor, "More Problems Arise with 'Black-Box Voting,'" *USA Today*, June 4, 2004.

26. Alexander Bolton, "Hagel's Ethics Filings Pose Disclosure Issue," *The Hill*, January 29, 2003, http://www.hillnews.com/news/ 012903/hagel.aspx.

27. Parallel monitoring provides a true test for Election Day fraud. Voting equipment is randomly selected on Election Day for testing

to ensure the equipment operates in accordance with approved preelection testing. These same machines then are tested again after the election to show that the software did not change because of date or time issues within the code. Parallel monitoring increasingly is being used by some states, including California and Washington, as part of their overall accountability efforts.

28. "On the Voting Machine Makers' Tab," *New York Times*, September 12, 2004, editorial.
29. See Habib Beary, "Gearing Up for India's Electronic Election," *BBC News.com*, February 27, 2004; and V. K. Raghunathan, "Voting in Indian Elections to Be Fully Electronic," *Straits Times* (Singapore), April 19, 2004.
30. Brit Williams made these comments in his talk and to me personally at the Voting Systems Testing Summit, November 28–29, 2005, Sacramento, California.
31. See the Commission on Federal Election Reforms report at www.american.edu/ia/cfer.

CHAPTER 2

1. Alex Keyssar, *The Right to Vote: The Contested History of Democracy in the United States* (New York: Basic Books, 2001), 2.
2. Jerry Fresia, *Toward an American Revolution: Exposing the Constitution and Other Illusions* (Boston: South End, 1988), 32.
3. This conversation was tape-recorded by Nixon's own hidden surveillance system that he had installed in the Oval Office. James Warren, "Some Vintage Nixon Saves the Day," *Chicago Tribune*, August 19, 2001.
4. David Paul Kuhn, "Voter Fraud Charges Out West," *CBSNews.com*, October 14, 2004, http://www.cbsnews.com/stories/2004/10/14/politics/main649380.shtml.
5. More than 400,000 voters called 866-MYVOTE1 and 866-OURVOTE reporting various election irregularities. Common Cause, "Report from the Voters: A First Look at 2004 Election Data," December 2004.
6. R. Michael Alvarez and Stephen Ansolabehere, "California Votes: The Promise of Election Day Registration," report published by Demos: A Network for Ideas in Action, 2002.
7. For example, Germany votes on a Sunday for its parliament and typically has voter turnout twice that of our congressional elections.

Puerto Rico makes Election Day a holiday and has a higher voter turnout than most of the 50 states.

8. Associated Press, "Sen. Clinton Pushes Voting Holiday, Allowing Ex-cons to Vote," *USA Today*, February 17, 2005.

9. The 11 nations are Australia, the Bahamas, Bangladesh, Barbados, Belize, India, Indonesia, Nauru, Samoa, the United Kingdom, and the United States. With the exception of Indonesia, all of the countries that do not grant a constitutional right to vote are former colonies of the British Empire. Thus, the lack of a constitutional right of suffrage is not the result of any brilliance on the part of the Founders and Framers of the Constitution; it is yet another legacy of 18th-century British colonialism.

10. See FairVote's website, http://www.fairvote.org/?page=837.

11. Tom Sherwood, "Hey, Let's Invade the District . . . ," *NBC4.com*, January 27, 2005.

12. Vanessa Gezari, "Go to Jail, Get to Vote—in Maine or Vermont," *St. Petersburg Times*, August 6, 2004, 1A; Justin Mason, "Vermont's Voting Laws Are Unique in Nation," *Vermont Brattleboro Reformer*, September 9, 2004.

13. Ann Louise Bardach, "How Florida Republicans Keep Blacks from Voting," *Los Angeles Times*, September 26, 2004.

14. "Nebraska in the Lead," *New York Times*, August 29, 2005, editorial.

15. BBC News, "Q&A: UK Prisoners' Right to Vote," October 6, 2005, http://news.bbc.co.uk/2/hi/uk_news/4316148.stm.

CHAPTER 3

1. Sam Smith, "Why Third Parties Matter," *The Progressive Review*, November 1, 1999.

2. See Francis Neely, Lisel Blash, and Corey Cook, "An Assessment of Ranked-Choice Voting in the San Francisco 2004 Election: Final Report," Public Research Institute, San Francisco State University, May 2005, http://pri.sfsu.edu/reports/SFSU-PRI_RCV_final_report_June_30.pdf.

3. Other online polls have had similarly strange results, courtesy of a plurality voting system that allowed a candidate to win with a low percentage of votes. For instance, when *Time* magazine held an Internet-based poll to choose its Man of the Century in 1999, Turkish ruler Mustafa Ataturk came in first, beating Franklin Roosevelt, Winston Churchill, Albert Einstein, Martin Luther King, and many others.

Notes

CHAPTER 4

1. In Illinois, the particular method of proportional representation used was known as *cumulative voting.*
2. The quotes from Illinois legislators Abner Mikva, Giddy Dyer, John Porter, Barbara Flynn Curie, Lee Daniels, and others are from hours of videotaped interviews conducted by the Center for Voting and Democracy and the Midwest Democracy Center.
3. Rick Pearson, "Political Ideology," *Chicago Tribune*, April 29, 2001.
4. "Better Politics from an Old Idea," *Chicago Tribune*, May 30, 1995, editorial.
5. "Let's Bring Back Old Way of Voting," *Chicago Sun-Times*, July 16, 2001, editorial.
6. Pearson, "Political Ideology."
7. See Christi Parsons, "New Legislature Reform Push," *Chicago Tribune*, July 8, 2001; and Steve Neal, "A Commonsense Plan to Revive Legislature," *Chicago Sun-Times*, July 11, 2001. Also see "Illinois Assembly on Political Representation and Alternative Electoral Systems," report by the Mikva-Edgar panel, Institute of Government and Public Affairs, University of Illinois, Spring 2001.
8. See FairVote, "Communities in America Currently Using Proportional Voting," http://www.fairvote.org/?page=243.
9. The "victory threshold" of representation for proportional voting is derived by making all contested seats in a multiseat district equal to the same number of votes. The threshold is calculated by dividing the (number of contested seats + 1) into 100 percent and adding one more vote to that number. Using this method, a three-seat district produces a victory threshold of 25 percent, plus one more vote.

$$\frac{100\% \text{ of total votes cast}}{\text{number of contested seats} + 1} = \frac{100\%}{3+1} = 25\% \ (+ 1 \text{ more vote})$$

   Qualitatively, this threshold, called the *Droop threshold*, is equal to the *minimum* number of votes a candidate needs to win such that, when all seats are filled, not enough votes are left over to elect another candidate. See the website of FairVote (http://www.fairvote.org) for additional resources about proportional representation.
10. David Lesher, "California's Great Disconnect: The Governed and the Government," *California Journal*, January 2005, 11.
11. Interestingly, the GOP gerrymanders in these five states alone give the Republicans most of their 15-seat majority in the House. In

Notes

Michigan, Pennsylvania, Florida, and Ohio, the Republicans and Democrats are essentially tied, statewide (as evidenced by Democrats recently winning presidential, gubernatorial and/or U.S. Senate statewide votes in Michigan, Pennsylvania, and Florida, and Kerry barely losing Ohio to Bush as Ohio Democrats won 49 percent of the statewide vote for U.S. House races). Yet the Republicans won two-thirds of the U.S. House seats in those four states (51 out of 77 races), mainly because of GOP-drawn districts. In Texas, Republicans won 58 percent of the statewide vote for U.S. House races but 66 percent of the seats. If the "votes to seats" distortions in these five states were balanced out, Democrats would gain approximately 14 seats, narrowing the House's Republican majority to about one vote.

12. See "A Good Proposal That Won't Do Much: If the Goal Is Reforming Elections, Neutral Panel Isn't Drastic Enough," *San Jose Mercury News*, March 31, 2005, editorial; "More Ideas for California: State's Situation Demands New Approaches," *Sacramento Bee*, January 1, 2004, editorial; and "Tired of Redistricting Hijinks? Try Statewide At-Large Elections," *Sacramento Bee*, December 14, 2003, editorial.

13. See William H. Frey, "Migration to the South Brings U.S. Blacks Full Circle," Population Reference Bureau, 2005, http://www.prb.org/Content/NavigationMenu/PT_articles/April-June_2001/Migration_to_the_South_Brings_U_S__Blacks_Full_Circle.htm. The South is now home to almost 55 percent of the country's blacks, compared with less than one-third of the U.S. Latino population and less than one-fifth of Asian Americans. Moreover, the lion's share of growth in the region's Latino population, 71 percent, occurred in two immigrant magnet states, Texas and Florida. The 15 other southern states gained 2.4 million blacks during the 1990s and only 1.4 million Latinos. Even including Texas and Florida, blacks make up 19 percent of the South's population; whites, 66 percent; and Latinos, only 12 percent.

14. Jeffrey McMurray, "Conservative Southern Dems Disappearing," Associated Press, April 25, 2005.

15. Robyn Followwill, "Cumulative Voting," *Amarillo Globe-News*, August 1, 1999.

16. See Robert Brischetto and Richard Engstrom, "Cumulative Voting and Latino Representation: Exit Surveys in Fifteen Texas Communities," *Social Science Quarterly* 78, no. 4 (1997).

Notes

17. By manipulating the victory threshold—the percentage of votes needed to win a seat—it is possible to fine-tune your democracy and decide how inclusive or exclusive you want it to be. If you want it to be extremely inclusive (and perhaps a bit fractious, with numerous parties that may not get along well), use a 1 percent threshold such as Israel used for many years. If you want your democracy to be exclusive, with few parties and few choices for voters, use a U.S.- or British-style winner-take-all system, with victory thresholds of 60 percent or higher for most legislative races. But experience around the world suggests a happy medium is possible, somewhere around Germany's 5 percent victory threshold or Ireland's 17 percent threshold.

18. This list is compiled by political scientist Mark Rush. See the table on the website of the Center for Voting and Democracy, http://www.fairvote.org/library/geog/europe/systems.htm.

19. "5 Provinces Consider Voting Changes," *Globe and Mail*, July 9, 2004. Also see the web site of the New America Foundation on Citizens Assemblies at www.newamerica.net/citizensassembly.

CHAPTER 5

1. Daniel Lazare, "Senatorial Privilege," *The American Prospect*, September 24–October 2, 2000.

2. *Baker v. Carr*, 369 U.S. 186 (1962) and *Reynolds v. Sims*, 377 U.S. 533 (1964), relied on the Fourteenth Amendment's Equal Protection Clause to ground this "one person, one vote" principle in the U.S. Constitution. They did *not*, however, establish that voters must be limited to having only one vote, as some have erroneously claimed. For instance, at-large plurality elections used in various state legislatures and city councils allow voters to cast multiple votes. But the key is that all voters receive the same number of votes and are treated equally, and therefore legally. Similarly, other electoral systems where voters cast more than one vote or rank multiple candidates, such as instant runoff voting, cumulative voting, and limited voting, are not violative of "one person, one vote" because all voters are treated equally.

3. See Center for Voting and Democracy, "Overview: Plurality Wins in Major American Elections, 1992–1998," October 2003, http://www.fairvote.org/plurality/collection1.htm. From 1992 to 1996, more U.S. Senate seats were won by plurality than had occurred

since the 1930s. A relatively high number of governors, too: Of 50 sitting governors, 22 won a plurality victory in the 1990s, including 15 in one of their general elections. Moreover, analyzing the election returns, we clearly see that the winner of several important races would have changed with the use of a majority voting system, as used in most presidential races around the world.

4. In Nebraska and Maine, a presidential candidate wins one electoral vote per each congressional district won and two electoral votes for winning the highest number of statewide votes (even if less than a majority). It's possible for Nebraska and Maine to split their electoral votes among two or more candidates, though that has never happened.

5. See FairVote/Center for Voting and Democracy, "The Shrinking Battleground: The 2008 Presidential Elections and Beyond," July 28, 2005, http://www.fairvote.org/presidential.

6. Statistics from FairVote/Center for Voting and Democracy, "The Shrinking Battleground."

7. New Mexico, Iowa, and Wisconsin also experienced close races, but their combined 22 electoral votes didn't add up to Florida's 27 and barely that of Ohio's 20 electoral votes.

8. Chris Pearson and Ryan O'Donnell, "The Shrinking Battleground," *TomPaine.com*, November 1, 2005.

9. Statistics from FairVote/Center for Voting and Democracy, "The Shrinking Battleground."

10. Jacob Hacker and Paul Pierson, *Off Center: The Republican Revolution and the Erosion of American Democracy* (New Haven and London: Yale University Press, 2005).

11. See Paul Rahe, "The Electoral College: A Defense," published by the Oklahoma Council of Public Affairs, http://www.ocpathink.org/Governance/TheElectoralCollegeDefense.html. A version of Rahe's article was published in the *American Spectator*, November 14, 2001.

12. See FairVote/Center for Voting and Democracy, "The Shrinking Battleground."

13. Robert Dahl, *How Democratic Is the American Constitution?* (New Haven, CT: Yale University Press, 2002), 74–76.

CHAPTER 6

1. Robert Dahl, *How Democratic Is the American Constitution?* (New Haven, CT: Yale University Press, 2002), 13.

2. Quote by Convention delegate James Wilson, from Dahl, *How Democratic Is the American Constitution?* 52.

Notes

3. Michael Lind, "75 Stars: How to Restore Democracy in the U.S. Senate (and End the Tyranny of Wyoming)," *Mother Jones*, January/February 1998, 47.
4. Dahl, *How Democratic Is the American Constitution?* 13–14.
5. Ibid., 13, 52–53.
6. Barry R. Weingast, "Political Stability and Civil War: Institutions, Commitment, and American Democracy," in *Analytical Narratives*, ed. Robert H. Bates, Avner Greif, Margaret Levi, Jean-Laurent Rosenthal, and Barry R. Weingast (Princeton, NJ: Princeton University Press, 1988), 148–93, 166, and 168. table 4.3; cited in Dahl, *How Democratic Is the American Constitution?* 53.
7. Frances E. Lee and Bruce I. Oppenheimer, *Sizing Up the Senate* (Chicago: University of Chicago Press, 1999), 4–5.
8. Ibid., 2.
9. Lind, "75 Stars," 46.
10. Farhad Manjoo, "Dump the Filibuster!" *Salon.com*, May 20, 2005.
11. Lee and Oppenheimer, *Sizing Up the Senate*, 118–20.
12. Matthew Soberg Shugart, "Filibuster Protects the Majority—of Voters," *San Diego Union Tribune*, May 18, 2005 (Shugart is a political scientist at University of California–San Diego); Hendrik Hertzberg, "Nuke 'Em," *New Yorker*, March 14, 2005; Manjoo, "Dump the Filibuster!"
13. See the tax table "Federal Outlays to States per Dollar of Tax Revenue Received," in *The World Almanac and Book of Facts, 2005* (New York: World Almanac Books, 2005), 158.
14. Lee and Oppenheimer, *Sizing Up the Senate*, 221.
15. John Lancaster, "Campaign Bill Unearths a Senate Relic: Debate," *Washington Post*, March 23, 2001, A1.
16. Mike Davis, *Magical Urbanism: Latinos Reinvent the U.S. Big City* (New York: Verso, 2000).
17. Richard N. Rosenfeld, "What Democracy? The Case for Abolishing the United States Senate," *Harper's*, May 1, 2004.
18. The World Economic Forum's ratings for both 2004–2005 and 2005–2006 ranked the world's most competitive economies as (1) Finland, (2) The United States, and (3) Sweden.
19. Rosenfeld, "What Democracy?"

CHAPTER 7

1. John Nichols and Robert W. McChesney, *It's the Media, Stupid* (New York: Seven Stories, 2000), 28.

Notes

2. Ted Turner, "My Beef with Big Media: How Government Protects Entertainment Giants—and Shuts Out Upstarts Like Me," *Washington Monthly*, July/August 2004.
3. Brooks Boliek, "Dixie Chicks' Radio Ban on Senate Panel Hit List," *HollywoodReporter.com*, July 9, 2003.
4. Anthony DeBarros, "Consolidation Changes Face of Radio," *USA Today*, July 7, 1998.
5. The FCC also wanted to allow corporations to own a newspaper and a TV station in the same market and permit corporations to own three TV stations in the largest markets, up from two, and two stations in medium-sized markets, up from one.
6. Turner, "My Beef with Big Media."
7. Frank Ahrens, "Powell Calls Rejection of Media Rules a Disappointment," *Washington Post*, June 29, 2004, E01.
8. Turner, "My Beef with Big Media."
9. Eric Brazil, "Micro-Radio No Small Battle," *San Francisco Examiner*, November 2, 2000, B-1.
10. Dan Morgan, "A Made-for-TV Windfall," *Washington Post*, May 2, 2000, A1.
11. Media analyst Thomas Wolzien of the investment house Sanford C. Bernstein & Co. has estimated the amount of public airwaves—and hence the subsidy to corporate broadcasters—to be $367 billion. See "Value of Public Airwaves Controlled by Broadcasters: $367 Billion, Analyst Says," *The Political Standard* 4, no. 3 (May 2001): 4, published by the Alliance for Better Campaigns, http://www.bettercampaigns.org.
12. Quoted in "Networks Skimped on Candidate, Issue Coverage during Campaign, Study Finds," *The Political Standard* 3, no. 9 (December 2000): 2.
13. Annenberg Public Policy Center of the University of Pennsylvania, "Are Voluntary Standards Working? Candidate Discourse on Network Evening News Programs," December 20, 2000, http://www.appcpenn.org. Also see "Networks Skimped," 1.
14. Gary Ruskin, "Disgusted by Politics on TV? Turn It Off," *Fort Worth Star-Telegram*, October 29, 2000.
15. Quoted in "Networks Skimped," 2.
16. This estimate was from an analysis by investment company Bear Stearns, cited in Alliance for Better Campaigns, "Gouging Democracy: How the Television Industry Profiteered on Campaign 2000," 2001, http://www.bettercampaigns.org, p. 4.

17. Ibid., p. 6.
18. Howard Kurtz, "Writer Backing Bush Plan Had Gotten Federal Contract," *Washington Post*, January 26, 2005, C1.
19. See World Policy Institute, "Otto J. Reich: Bad for Latin America," Arms Trade Resource Center, Current Update, April 9, 2001, http://www.worldpolicy.org/projects/arms/updates/ottoreich.htm.
20. Eric Schmitt, "Military Admits Planting News in Iraq," *New York Times*, December 3, 2005; Jeff Gerth, "Military's Information War Is Vast and Often Secretive," *New York Times*, December 11, 2005.
21. Matt Kelley, "Pentagon Rolls Out Stealth PR: $300M Effort Aims to Spread Pro-U.S. Messages in Foreign Media," *USA Today*, December 14, 2005, 1A.
22. Here are just a few of the front-page *New York Times* headlines for "scoops" that Judith Miller landed before and after the invasion that have since been discredited: "U.S. Says Hussein Intensifies Quest for A-Bomb Parts"; "Illicit Arms Kept till Eve of War, an Iraqi Scientist Is Said to Assert"; "U.S. Analysts Link Iraq Labs to Germ Arms"; "Iraqi Tells of Renovations at Sites for Chemical and Nuclear Arms." See Joe Conason, "Embedded over Her Head in Washington," *New York Observer*, August 23, 2005.
23. "The *Times* and Iraq," *New York Times*, May 26, 2004, editorial. The *Times* wrote, "[W]e have found a number of instances of coverage that was not as rigorous as it should have been . . . information that was controversial then, and seems questionable now, was insufficiently qualified or allowed to stand unchallenged."
24. Paul Krugman, "Behind the Great Divide," *New York Times*, February 18, 2003.
25. Peter Johnson, "Amanpour: CNN Practiced Self-Censorship," *USA Today*, September 15, 2003.
26. Alan B. Krueger, "Fair? Balanced? A Study Finds It Does Not Matter," *New York Times*, August 18, 2005.
27. See Owen M. Fiss, *The Irony of Free Speech* (Cambridge, MA: Harvard University Press, 1996).
28. See *Turner Broadcasting System v. Federal Communications Commission*, 520 U.S. 180 (1997).
29. Turner, "My Beef with Big Media."
30. For many years, television and radio stations were required to give equal time to opposing sides of public or political issues to ensure the American public heard all sides of a debate. It was a requirement made by the Federal Communications Commission that

Notes

came to be known as the Fairness Doctrine. But in 1986, a federal court ruled that the Fairness Doctrine did not have the force of law and could be overturned without congressional approval. Congress passed a bill to make the doctrine law, but the bill was vetoed by President Reagan in 1987, and the Fairness Doctrine was abolished. Since then, the country has experienced a proliferation of highly partisan news outlets that disseminate unbalanced news coverage.

31. See McKinsey & Company, "Review of Public Service Broadcasting around the World," September 2004, http://www.ofcom.org.uk/consult/condocs/psb2/psb2/psbwp/wp3mck.pdf.
32. See the report by NPR Ombudsman Jeffrey A. Dvorkin, "NPR: Mysteries of the Organization, Part I," December 14, 2005, http://www.npr.org/templates/story/story.php?storyId=5053335.
33. See Charter and Agreement of the British Broadcasting Corporation located at http://www.bbc.co.uk/info/policies/charter/
34. Henry Milner, *Civic Literacy: How Informed Citizens Make Democracy Work* (Hanover, NH: University Press of New England, 2002), 98–104.
35. Ibid.
36. BuzzFlash interview: Robert W. McChesney, "Working to Reclaim Our Free Press," May 2005.
37. John Borland, "Estonia Sets Shining Wi-Fi Example," *CNetNews.com*, November 1, 2005, http://news.com.com/Estonia+sets+shining+Wi-Fi+example/2010-7351_3-5924673.html?tag=html.alert.
38. Drew Clark, "City-Driven Network War in the City of Brotherly Love," *National Journal*, August 22, 2005.

CHAPTER 8

1. Thomas B. Edsall and Derek Willis, "Fundraising Records Broken by Both Major Political Parties," *Washington Post*, December 3, 2004, A07.
2. Bill O'Reilly made this comment during an interview on *The Daily Show with Jon Stewart.*
3. *Buckley v. Valeo*, 424 U.S. 1 (1976)
4. California Public Interest Research Group (PIRG), "Sacramento for Sale," http://www.pirg.org/calpirg/reports/sactoforsale.html. Also, press release from the Center for Responsive Politics dated November 8, 2000; see http://www.crp.org.

5. For information on women and minority participation in the primaries, compare these two reports: The Clean Elections Institute, Inc., "2004 Election Statistics," http://azclean.org/documents/1-21-05Gen.Elect.Statistics2.doc; and Hector J. Preciado, "Funding Our Own Democracy: A Study of the Effects of Public Funding on Minority Candidates and Voters," Greenlining Institute, Summer 2002, http://greenlining.org/uploads/pdfs/1112164221-funding ourowndemocracy.pdf, p. 8.
6. Those three races were the ones won by Deborrah Simpson, a waitress and single mom who had never run for office; 68-year-old Marilyn Canavan; and Green Party candidate John Eder.
7. Timothy Werner and Kenneth Mayer, "The Impact of Public Election Funding on Women Candidates: Comparative Evidence from State Elections," a paper prepared for the Midwest Political Science Association, April 7, 2005, http://campfin.polisci.wisc.edu/ Gender%20and%20Public%20Funding.pdf.
8. See Preciado, "Funding Our Own Democracy."
9. *OUCH! A Regular Bulletin on How Money in Politics Hurts You*, no. 49, May 18, 2000.
10. Jacob Hacker and Paul Pierson, *Off Center: The Republican Revolution and the Erosion of American Democracy* (New Haven, CT: Yale University Press, 2005), 142.
11. Elizabeth Drew, *Showdown: The Struggle between the Gingrich Congress and the Clinton White House* (New York: Simon & Schuster, 1996), 116.
12. Mark Sherman, "Abramoff Pleads Guilty, Will Cooperate," Associated Press, January 3, 2006.
13. Sam Smith, "Why Third Parties Matter," *The Progressive Review*, November 1, 1999.
14. Paul Taylor and Norman Ornstein, "The Case for Free Air Time—Issue Brief," New America Foundation, June 1, 2002, http://www.newamerica.net/index.cfm?pg=article&DocID=894.

CHAPTER 9

1. Joan Biskupic, "Election Still Splits Court," *USA Today*, January 22, 2001, 1.
2. Dan Balz and Helen Dewar, "Analysis: Certification Brings Anything but Certainty," *Washington Post*, November 26, 2000, A1; also see Eric Pianin and Juliet Eilperin, "Angry Hill Republicans

Would Reject Gore Presidency," *Washington Post*, November 20, 2000, A8.

3. Two witnesses described this extraordinary scene to *Newsweek*. See Evan Thomas and Michael Isikoff, "The Truth behind the Pillars," *Newsweek*, December 25, 2000, 46.

4. Amar quoted in Vincent Bugliosi, "None Dare Call It Treason," *The Nation*, February 5, 2001.

5. Ibid.

6. Biskupic, "Election Still Splits Court," 2.

7. Thomas and Isikoff, "The Truth behind the Pillars," 48.

8. Charles Levendosky, "Supreme Court Invites Criticism," *Progressive Populist*, March 1, 2001.

9. Anonymous *per curiam* (Latin for "by the court") opinions are almost always issued for unanimous (9–0) opinions in relatively unimportant and uncontroversial cases, or where justices wish to be very brief. But as *USA Today* pointed out, "Neither was the case here." Bugliosi, "None Dare Call It Treason."

10. *Bush v. Gore*, 531 U.S. 98, 121 S.Ct. 525, December 12, 2000, pp. 10–11. See David E. Rosenbaum, "Seeking a Formula for Voting Laws," *New York Times*, December 20, 2000, A17.

11. Opinion poll conducted of 1,000 likely voters, October 29–30, 2005, by Rasmussen Reports. See http://rasmussenreports.com/ 2005/Supreme%20Court%20Favs%20Oct%2031.htm.

12. Statistics from Northwestern University law professors Steven Calabresi and James Lindgren, cited in Bruce Bartlett, ". . . and Tenure Traps," *Washington Times*, July 6, 2005.

13. Ibid.

14. Judith Resnik, "Judicial Selection, Independent Jurists, and Life-Tenure?" http://jurist.law.pitt.edu/forum/symposium-jc/resnik.php.

15. Norman J. Ornstein, "To Break the Stalemate, Give Judges Less Than Life," *Washington Post*, November 28, 2004.

16. John M. Broder and Carolyn Marshall, "White House Memos Offer Opinions on Supreme Court," *New York Times*, July 30, 2005, A11.

17. Bartlett, ". . . and Tenure Traps."

18. Doug Cassel, "The Judicial Filibuster—How Other Democracies Protect Minority Rights," Chicago Public Radio, May 25, 2005, http://chicagopublicradio.org/programs/worldview/transcripts/ 20050525.asp.

19. Cassel, "The Judicial Filibuster."

20. Frances E. Lee and Bruce I. Oppenheimer, *Sizing Up the Senate* (Chicago: University of Chicago Press, 1999), 118–20.
21. Mark Tushnet, *A Court Divided* (London: Norton, 2005), 9.
22. Voting record comparison is for the years 1994–2004. *New York Times,* http://www.nytimes.com/packages/html/politics/20050701_ NOMINATION_GRAPHIC/index_02.html.
23. Ruth Marcus, "The Ginsburg Fallacy," *Washington Post,* November 15, 2005, A21.
24. Jamin B. Raskin, *Overruling Democracy: The Supreme Court vs. The American People* (New York: Routledge, 2003), 4.
25. See People for the American Way, "Courting Disaster: An Update Examining the 2001–2002 Term," July 2, 2002.
26. Judith Resnik and Theodore Ruger, "One Robe, Two Hats," *New York Times,* July 17, 2005
27. Ibid.
28. On September 14, 2005, Senators Herb Kohl (D-WI) and Sam Brownback (R-KS) each asked one brief question to the nominee about the chief justice's role overseeing this vast federal judicial bureaucracy. Brownback's question had to do with whether Roberts believed Congress had the authority to split the Ninth Circuit Court of Appeal into two separate courts. Roberts replied in the affirmative. Kohl's question was rambling and unfocused, and he received a similarly rambling and unfocused reply.

CHAPTER 10

1. Yvonne Lee, "America's Home Land Security—A Color Coded Response?" *Sing Tao Daily,* September 5, 2005.
2. Ronald Reagan, "First Inaugural Address," January 20, 1981.
3. Grover Norquist made this statement to a National Public Radio (NPR) interviewer, and it was broadcast in an NPR profile of Norquist done by newscaster Mara Liasson for Bob Edwards's show in May 2001.
4. Marvin Meyers, ed., *The Mind of the Founder: Sources of the Political Thought of James Madison* (New York: Bobbs-Merrill, 1973), 523, 525, 530.
5. Alexis de Tocqueville, *Democracy in America* (New York: New American Library, 1956), 104.
6. James Arnold, "Echoes of Enron in Telecoms' Collapse," *BBCNews.com,* February 11, 2002.

7. See "Enron Named #22 of '100 Best Companies to Work For in America,'" press release from Enron Corp., December 18, 2000, http://www.csrwire.com/article.cgi/525.html.
8. Jeff Plungis, "Bill Curbs SUV Tax Write-off," *Detroit News*, October 7, 2004. In 2004, Congress trimmed the loophole from $100,000 to $25,000, but it created other loopholes, including a "bonus depreciation." Currently, a business owner purchasing a Hummer H1 (for $106,185) would be able to deduct $60,722 in the first year under the revised rules: a $25,000 equipment deduction, $24,356 in bonus depreciation, and $11,366 in regular depreciation. Also see Mark Solheim, "Heavy Metal," *Kiplinger's Personal Finance*, September 2003.
9. Phillip Longman, "The Best Care Anywhere," *Washington Monthly*, January 1, 2005.
10. George Bush's national coordinator for health care information technology, Dr. David Brailer, estimates that if the U.S. health care system as a whole would adopt electronic medical records and computerized prescription orders, it would save as much as 2 percent of the gross domestic product and also dramatically improve the quality of care.
11. Paul Glastris, "Bush's Ownership Society: Why No One's Buying," *Washington Monthly*, December 2005.
12. Ibid.

CONCLUSION

1. Alexis de Tocqueville, *Democracy in America* (New York: New American Library, 1956), 104.
2. Charles Krauthammer, "In Praise of Low Voter Turnout," *Time*, May 21, 1990.
3. William G. Sinnigen and Arthur E. R. Boak, *A History of Rome to A.D. 565* (New York: Macmillan, 1977), 68, 70–72, 78.
4. The eight states where Democrats have total control over government are New Mexico, Illinois, New Jersey, Washington, West Virginia, Maine, North Carolina, and Louisiana. The seven states with Democratic-controlled legislatures and moderate Republican governors are Rhode Island, Vermont, Hawaii, Massachusetts, California, Maryland, and Connecticut.

Acknowledgments

For the past 15 years, I have worn the dual hats of political analyst and political reformer, dividing my time between writing books and op-eds while at the same time running political campaigns to enact electoral reform. During that time period, I have worked with, learned from, and been inspired by an amazing array of dedicated people selflessly driven by no desire or personal ambition other than to see our United States of America live up to its own great traditions and lofty rhetoric. Many of these people have become my friends and colleagues, and I am proud and gratified to know them. It is not possible to name them all, but I would be remiss if I did not single out a few.

Rob Richie, my former colleague and cofounder at the Center for Voting and Democracy (now known as FairVote), is at the top of the list. For many years, Rob and I worked shoulder to shoulder, trying to drag American democracy away from the cliff at which it finds itself. Rob has shown patient leadership, produced ground-breaking scholarship, and helped reformat our understanding of American politics. As we have learned, progress comes in small steps.

My new colleagues at the New America Foundation, including Ted Halstead, David Lesher, Sherle Schwenninger, Mike Lind, and Mark Schmitt, have added immeasurably to my understanding of the importance of the American political center, and they have afforded me the support to continue this important work.

I am deeply grateful to fellow reformers who assisted me with successful campaigns in San Francisco to pass both instant runoff voting and public financing of campaigns, including Caleb Kleppner, Matt Gonzalez, Ross Mirkarimi, Tom Ammiano, Mark Leno, Dan Johnson-Weinberger, Howard Wallace, Rob Arnow, Boris Delepine, Susan King, Charles Kalish, Lucy

Acknowledgments

Colvin, Robert Haaland, Bill Redpath, David Wilner, Joan Mandel, Jim Knox, Joann Fuller, Richard DeLeon, Anne Bink and her wonderful Syracuse friends, Steve Chessin, Jim Lindsay, Pete Martineau, Paula Lee, Joe Moore, Rosalinda Guillen, Dave Kadlecek, Maritza Valenzuela, Medea Benjamin, Dave Grenell, Eric Mar, Dave Heller, Barbara Blong, Betty Traynor, and several others, too many to list.

I am also indebted to many other people across the United States who have cared enough about the state of American democracy to give freely of their time, energy, and resources, notably John B. Anderson, Hendrik Hertzberg, Lani Guinier, Ed Still, Katrina vanden Heuvel, Ralph Nader, Theresa Amato, Phil Tajitsu Nash, Chris Jerdonek, Rob Dickinson, Janet Anderson, Herm Ross, Tony Solgard, Lester Goldstein, Dorka Keehn, Brent White, Krist Novoselic, Terry Bouricius, Kenny Mostern, Eric Olson, John Nichols, Bob McChesney, Mike Feinstein, John Koza, Dolores Huerta, David Cobb, Jamie Raskin, Derek Cressman, Matthew Cossolotto, Tabitha Hall, Amy Connolly, Kevin McKeown, John Gear, Blair Bobier, George Pillsbury, Lynne Serpe, Malia Lazu, Doug Amy, Paul Turner, Roy Ulrich, Kathay Feng, Tory Griffith, Nick Nyhart, Micah Sifry, Arianna Huffington, Jim Hightower, Trevor Potter, Lee Mortimer, Howie Fain, Chip Wagoner, Ken Jacobus, Joel Rogers, John Bonifaz, Harriet Barlow, Rashad Robinson, Fred McBride, Bill Greider, Peter Vickery, Jesse Jackson Jr., Cynthia McKinney, Mel Watt, James Clyburn, Antonio Gonzalez, Arend Lijphart, Matthew Shugart, Dick Engstrom, Kathy Barber, and the many other great people out there who believe enough in our country to try to make it better.

Our efforts here in the United States have been aided by political reformers in other countries, most notably by Ken Ritchie from the Electoral Reform Society and Peter Facey from the New Politics Network in the United Kingdom, Professor Ben Reilly in Australia, Professor Henry Milner in Canada and Sweden,

Acknowledgments

and Larry Gordon from FairVote Canada. Also a very dear thank-you to the whole world's good friend, and mine, Rod Donald, a member of the New Zealand Parliament and electoral reformer who passed away unexpectedly at the age of 48, in the prime of his life and political accomplishments. Rod, you are dearly missed—you left us much too soon.

I also wish to thank the marvelous crew at PoliPointPress, including Scott Jordan, Rhoda Dunn, Carol Pott, Michael Bass, and Laura Larson. A special note of gratitude to my editor, Peter Richardson, whose patience, thoughtful remarks, and discerning eye made the manuscript leaner and truer to its mark.

And, of course, once again I must thank my partner Lucy Colvin for her astute comments about the manuscript, for her patient love, support, and help in keeping me in the saddle not only during the writing of this book but for all these years, and for keeping it fun along the way. Without you, I'm not sure any of this would be possible.

Here's to a hopeful future with a renewed democracy in the United States.

Steven Hill
San Francisco
May 2006

Index

Index

Cable TV, 130
California
    ballot initiative to give redistricting
        to independent commission,
        74–76
    demographic changes, 71
    partisan residential patterns, 72–73
    political crisis in, 71–73
    presidential election results (2004),
        72–73
    proportional representation plan
        for, 76–79
    underrepresentation in Senate, 108
    voter registration in, 39
    voting equipment purchases, 25
Californians for Electoral Reform, 62
California Voter Foundation, 33
Caltech-MIT study, 17
Campaign finance
    presidential election (2004), 137
    and proportional representation
        system, 69
    quid pro quo problem, 143–146
    reform, 138–143, 148–151
Campaign Legal Center, 152
Campaigns
    lack of issues, 9, 11
    media coverage, 121–124
    negative campaigning, 55–56
    strategies, 56, 93
Campbell, Tom, 195
Canada
    Citizens Assembly, 85–87
    mandatory retirement age for
        justices, 159–160
Capitol building, ceiling fresco
    saying, 11
Carter, Jimmy, 5, 32, 41, 195
Carter-Baker Commission, 32
Casalino, Lawrence, 178
Casey, William, 124
Cassel, Doug, 160
Censorship, of news, 10, 128–129
Census Bureau, 12, 113

Center for Digital Democracy, 130,
    135
Center for Media and Public Affairs,
    122, 135
Center for Voting and Democracy, 63
Cheney, Dick, 164
Chicago *Sun-Times*, 69
Chicago Tribune, 69
Chief justice, of Supreme Court,
    administrative and judicial
    powers of, 164–167
Ciber, Inc., 25
Cisneros, Henry, 179
Cities
    campaign finance reform, 142–143
    proportional voting in, 81–82
Citizens Assemblies, 85–87
Civil Rights Commission, 47
"Clean money," 146–147
Clear Channel, 8, 118, 119, 120
Clinton, Bill, 50, 111, 170, 179
Clinton, Hillary, 41, 195
CNN, 10, 126
Comcast, 130, 134
Commission, for national elections,
    28–30
Common Cause, 74, 103
Communications Act (1934), 121,
    133, 151
Computerized voting, 4, 18, 23–24, 30
Connecticut, public financing of
    campaigns, 149
Conservation, 12
Conservatives, 2, 13–14, 131, 162,
    170
Constitutional amendment proposals
    abolishment of Electoral College,
        102
    right-to-vote, 42
Constitutional Convention, 97, 105
Consumer debt, 12–13
Conyers, John, 21
Corporate campaign contributions,
    143–144

Index

Index

Index

Index

Index

Index

229

Index

Index

Wolzien, Thomas, 210n11
Women
  in House of Representatives,
    199n17
  and proportional representation
    system, 68
  in Senate, 109

Woodward, Bob, 10, 125
Working Families Party, 88
Wyle Laboratories, 25
Wyoming, voter registration in, 40

Zogby poll, 2

About the Author

Steven Hill is the director of the Political Reform Program of the New America Foundation and cofounder of FairVote/Center for Voting and Democracy. His articles and commentaries have appeared in dozens of newspapers and magazines, including the *New York Times, Washington Post, Los Angeles Times, Wall Street Journal, Christian Science Monitor, The Nation, Ms., San Francisco Chronicle, San Jose Mercury News, Salon.com, Roll Call, American Prospect, New York Daily News, Miami Herald, Baltimore Sun, Chicago Tribune, Houston Chronicle,* and many others.

His book *Fixing Elections: The Failure of America's Winner Take All Politics* has been called "the most important book on American democracy that has come out in many years." He has lectured widely in the United States and Europe, and has appeared on C-SPAN, Fox News, National Public Radio, and numerous radio and TV programs across the nation and in Europe.

Hill was campaign manager of San Francisco's successful effort that passed instant runoff voting for local offices, and he was one of the organizers of San Francisco's successful efforts to enact public financing of campaigns for local elections.

The Blue Pages: A Directory of Companies Rated by Their Politics and Practices

Fed up with pay-to-play politics? Ready to do something about it? This handy pocket directory rates companies by their political contributions and describes their business practices. Quick access to over 4,000 listings helps consumers vote with their wallets by purchasing from companies that share their political and social values.

ISBN 0-9760621-1-9 $9.95

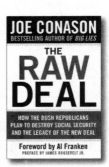

The Raw Deal: How the Bush Republicans Plan to Destroy Social Security and the Legacy of the New Deal

By Joe Conason. Foreword by Al Franken.
Preface by James Roosevelt Jr.

"With insight and clarity, Joe Conason shows how the long-standing conservative antipathy toward Social Security has morphed into a lavishly funded and breathtakingly dishonest conservative PR campaign...In untangling spools of GOP propaganda, The Raw Deal sets the record straight and shows what's really at stake for all Americans in the current battle." **David Brock, President and CEO, Media Matters for America, and author of** *Blinded by the Right*

ISBN: 0-9760621-2-7 $11.00

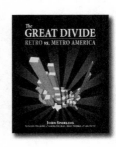

The Great Divide: Retro vs. Metro America

By John Sperling, Suzanne Helburn, Samuel George, John Morris, and Carl Hunt

"John Sperling has brilliantly exposed the truth about Retro Republicans using fear to marginalize America's quest for fairness and social justice. Yet, as the book shows, there is a real Metro progressive majority in the country that can create a 'more perfect union'. It needs to speak up and take action. It can't happen soon enough." **Arianna Huffington, columnist, political commentator and bestselling author of** *Pigs at the Trough*

ISBN: 0-9760621-0-0 $19.95

Available at booksellers everywhere
Visit us at PoliPointPress.org